PSSA 5 Math Practice Book 2020

Extra Exercises and Two Full Length PSSA Math Tests to Ace the Exam

By

Michael Smith & Reza Nazari

PSSA 5 Math Practice Book 2020

Published in the United State of America By

The Math Notion

Web: WWW.MathNotion.com

Email: info@Mathnotion.com

About the Author

Michael Smith has been a math instructor for over a decade now. He holds a master's degree in Management. Since 2006, Michael has devoted his time to both teaching and developing exceptional math learning materials. As a Math instructor and test prep expert, Michael has worked with thousands of students. He has used the feedback of his students to develop a unique study program that can be used by students to drastically improve their math score fast and effectively.

– SAT Math Comprehensive Exercise Book

– ACT Math Comprehensive Exercise Book

– ISEE Math Comprehensive Exercise Book

– SSAT Math Comprehensive Exercise Book

–many Math Education Workbooks, Exercise Books and Study Guides

As an experienced Math teacher, Mr. Smith employs a variety of formats to help students achieve their goals: He tutors online and in person, he teaches students in large groups, and he provides training materials and textbooks through his website and through Amazon.

You can contact Michael via email at:

info@Mathnotion.com

This book is your ticket to ace the PSSA Math Test!

PSSA Math Practice Book 2020, which reflects the 2020 test guidelines and topics, provides students with confidence and math skills they need to succeed on the PSSA Math test. After completing this workbook, PSSA Math test takers will have solid foundation and adequate practice that is necessary to ace the PSSA Math test.

This updated version of the book offers a complete review of the PSSA Math test, including:

- Arithmetic and Number Operations
- Algebra and Functions,
- Geometry and Measurement
- Data analysis, Statistics, & Probability
- … and also includes **two full-length practice tests!**

This comprehensive PSSA Math practice book contains many exciting features to help you prepare for the PSSA Math test, including:

- Content 100% aligned with the 2020 PSSA test
- Provided and tested by PSSA Math test experts
- Dynamic design and easy-to-follow activities
- Targeted, skill-building practices
- Complete coverage of all PSSA Math topics which you will be tested
- 2 complete and realistic PSSA Math practice tests with detailed answers and explanations

WWW.MathNotion.com

... So Much More Online!

✓ FREE Math Lessons

✓ More Math Learning Books!

✓ Mathematics Worksheets

✓ Online Math Tutors

For a PDF Version of This Book

Please Visit WWW.MathNotion.com

contents

Chapter 1:

Place Values and Number Sense

Topics that you'll practice in this chapter:

✓ Place Values

✓ Compare Numbers

✓ Numbers in Word

✓ Rounding

✓ Odd or Even

Place Values

✍ **Write numbers in expanded form.**

1) Thirty–six $30 + 6$

2) Sixty–five   ___ + ___

3) Fifty–three   ___ + ___

4) Eighty–two   ___ + ___

5) Ninety–three   ___ + ___

6) Twenty–four   ___ + ___

7) Seventy –four   ___ + ___

8) sixty –one   ___ + ___

9) Ninety–six   ___ + ___

10) Eighty –eight   ___ + ___

11) Thirty –nine   ___ + ___

✍ **Circle the correct choice.**

12) The 6 in 96 is in the	ones place	tens place	hundreds place
13) The 3 in 36 is in the	ones place	tens place	hundreds place
14) The 3 in 963 is in the	ones place	tens place	hundreds place
15) The 0 in 704 is in the	ones place	tens place	hundreds place
16) The 8 in 865 is in the	ones place	tens place	hundreds place

Comparing and Ordering Numbers

✎ **Use less than, equal to or greater than.**

1) 36 _____ 56

2) 83 _____ 99

3) 62 _____ 46

4) 65 _____ 63

5) 97 _____ 97

6) 39 _____ 32

7) 81 _____ 78

8) 50 _____ 43

9) 68 _____ 68

10) 83 _____ 86

11) 46 _____ 59

12) 79 _____ 68

13) 99 _____ 78

14) 45 _____ 35

✎ **Order each set of integers from least to greatest.**

15) 15, −13, −8, −5, 9   ___, ___, ___, ___, ___, ___

16) −5, −15, 3, 13, 8   ___, ___, ___, ___, ___, ___

17) 27, −22, −25, 30, −36   ___, ___, ___, ___, ___, ___

18) −15, −35, 32, −8, 52   ___, ___, ___, ___, ___, ___

19) 47, −43, 39, −12, 45   ___, ___, ___, ___, ___, ___

20) 98, 66, −39, 67, −44   ___, ___, ___, ___, ___, ___

✎ **Order each set of integers from greatest to least.**

21) 20, 24, −12, −24, −18   ___, ___, ___, ___, ___, ___

22) 36, 46, −19, −30, 59   ___, ___, ___, ___, ___, ___

23) 65, −51, −38, 67, −20   ___, ___, ___, ___, ___, ___

24) 88, 91, −34, −30, 84   ___, ___, ___, ___, ___, ___

25) −15, 86, −26, −73, 54   ___, ___, ___, ___, ___, ___

26) −86, −55, −60, 38, 59   ___, ___, ___, ___, ___, ___

Write Numbers in Words

✍ Write each number in words.

1) 192 _____

2) 311 _____

3) 551 _____

4) 464 _____

5) 807 _____

6) 719 _____

7) 175 _____

8) 236 _____

9) 908 _____

10) 1,630 _____

11) 1,147 _____

12) 5,374 _____

13) 2,481 _____

14) 1,676 _____

15) 5,240 _____

16) 1,365 _____

17) 5,010 _____

Odd or Even

✍ **Identify whether each number is even or odd.**

1) 18 _____   7) 32 _____

2) 7 _____   8) 67 _____

3) 13 _____   9) 96 _____

4) 28 _____   10) 16 _____

5) 33 _____   11) 88 _____

6) 17 _____   12) 79 _____

✍ **Circle the even number in each group.**

13) 28, 33, 55, 13, 17, 69

14) 11, 19, 87, 53, 33, 86

15) 21, 67, 18, 47, 65, 39

16) 97, 96, 73, 83, 23, 67

✍ **Circle the odd number in each group.**

17) 16, 18, 44, 64, 55, 98

18) 18, 26, 28, 22, 32, 97

19) 48, 84, 87, 94, 62, 58

20) 23, 18, 52, 32, 68, 78

Rounding Numbers

✍ Round each number to the nearest ten.

1) 24	5) 14	9) 47
2) 98	6) 39	10) 63
3) 43	7) 84	11) 79
4) 27	8) 90	12) 66

✍ Round each number to the nearest hundred.

13) 196	17) 243	21) 682
14) 263	18) 332	22) 584
15) 738	19) 278	23) 863
16) 118	20) 938	24) 498

✍ Round each number to the nearest thousand.

25) 1,252	29) 8,048	33) 61,890
26) 2,870	30) 63,637	34) 81,170
27) 5,346	31) 28,432	35) 65,730
28) 4,579	32) 12,936	36) 46,635

Answers of Worksheets – Chapter 1

Place Values

1) 30+6
2) 60+5
3) 50+3
4) 80+2
5) 90+3
6) 20+4
7) 70+4
8) 60+1
9) 90+6
10) 80+8
11) 30+9
12) ones place
13) tens place
14) ones place
15) tens place
16) hundreds place

Comparing and Ordering Numbers

1) 36 less than 56
2) 83 less than 99
3) 62 greater than 46
4) 65 greater than 63
5) 97 equals to 97
6) 39 greater than 32
7) 81 greater than 78
8) 50 greater than 43
9) 68 equals to 68
10) 83 less than 86
11) 46 less than 59
12) 79 greater than 68
13) 99 greater than 78
14) 45 greater than 35
15) $-13, -8, -5, 9, 15$
16) $-15, -5, 3, 8, 13$
17) $-36, -25, -22, 27, 30$
18) $-35, -15, -8, 32, 52$
19) $-43, -12, 39, 45, 47$
20) $-44, -39, 66, 67, 98$
21) $24, 20, -12, -18, -24$
22) $59, 46, 36, -19, -30$
23) $67, 65, -20, -38, -51$
24) $91, 88, 84, -30, -34$
25) $86, 54, -15, -26, -73$
26) $59, 38, -55, -60, -86$

Write Numbers in Words

1) One hundred ninety-two
2) Three hundred eleven
3) Five hundred fifty-one
4) Four hundred sixty-four
5) Eight hundred seven
6) Seven hundred nineteen
7) one hundred seventy-fifty
8) Two hundred thirty-six
9) Nine hundred eight
10) One thousand, six hundred thirty
11) One thousand, 0ne hundred forty-seven
12) Five thousand, three hundred seventy-four
13) Two thousand, four hundred eighty-one
14) one thousand, six hundred seventy-six

15) Five thousand, two hundred forty

17) Five thousand, ten

16) one thousand, three hundred sixty-five

Odd or Even

1) Even	6) Odd	11) Even	16)
2) Odd	7) Even	12) Odd	17)
3) Odd	8) Odd	13)	18)
4) Even	9) Even	14)	19)
5) Odd	10) Even	15)	20)

Rounding Numbers

1) 20	13) 200	25) 1,000
2) 100	14) 300	26) 3,000
3) 40	15) 700	27) 5,000
4) 30	16) 100	28) 5,000
5) 10	17) 200	29) 8,000
6) 40	18) 300	30) 64,000
7) 80	19) 300	31) 28,000
8) 90	20) 900	32) 13,000
9) 50	21) 700	33) 62,000
10) 60	22) 600	34) 81,000
11) 80	23) 900	35) 66,000
12) 70	24) 500	36) 47,000

Chapter 2:
Adding and Subtracting

Topics that you'll practice in this chapter:

✓ Adding Two–Digit Numbers

✓ Subtracting Two–Digit Numbers

✓ Adding Three–Digit Numbers

✓ Adding Hundreds

✓ Adding 4–Digit Numbers

✓ Subtracting 4–Digit Numbers

✓ Estimate Sums

✓ Estimate Differences

Adding Two–Digit Numbers

✐ **Find each sum.**

1) $\begin{array}{r} 50 \\ + 18 \\ \hline \end{array}$

2) $\begin{array}{r} 32 \\ + 34 \\ \hline \end{array}$

3) $\begin{array}{r} 46 \\ + 21 \\ \hline \end{array}$

4) $\begin{array}{r} 32 \\ + 32 \\ \hline \end{array}$

5) $\begin{array}{r} 65 \\ + 20 \\ \hline \end{array}$

6) $\begin{array}{r} 44 \\ + 25 \\ \hline \end{array}$

7) $\begin{array}{r} 89 \\ + 6 \\ \hline \end{array}$

8) $\begin{array}{r} 53 \\ + 12 \\ \hline \end{array}$

9) $\begin{array}{r} 70 \\ + 30 \\ \hline \end{array}$

10) $\begin{array}{r} 44 \\ + 12 \\ \hline \end{array}$

11) $\begin{array}{r} 50 \\ + 22 \\ \hline \end{array}$

12) $\begin{array}{r} 39 \\ + 18 \\ \hline \end{array}$

13) $\begin{array}{r} 29 \\ + 35 \\ \hline \end{array}$

14) $\begin{array}{r} 49 \\ + 21 \\ \hline \end{array}$

15) $\begin{array}{r} 65 \\ + 33 \\ \hline \end{array}$

16) $\begin{array}{r} 63 \\ + 30 \\ \hline \end{array}$

17) $\begin{array}{r} 66 \\ + 26 \\ \hline \end{array}$

18) $\begin{array}{r} 58 \\ + 23 \\ \hline \end{array}$

Subtracting Two–Digit Numbers

✎ **Find each difference.**

1)
$$26 \\ -20$$

2)
$$70 \\ -26$$

3)
$$97 \\ -37$$

4)
$$38 \\ -21$$

5)
$$63 \\ -22$$

6)
$$79 \\ -30$$

7)
$$89 \\ -42$$

8)
$$96 \\ -28$$

9)
$$77 \\ -31$$

10)
$$78 \\ -27$$

11)
$$79 \\ -36$$

12)
$$46 \\ -21$$

13)
$$78 \\ -39$$

14)
$$69 \\ -46$$

15)
$$49 \\ -21$$

16)
$$93 \\ -21$$

17)
$$69 \\ -45$$

18)
$$96 \\ -63$$

Adding Three–Digit Numbers

✎ **Find each sum.**

1)
$$
\begin{array}{r}
526 \\
+\ 36 \\
\hline
\end{array}
$$

2)
$$
\begin{array}{r}
725 \\
+\ 130 \\
\hline
\end{array}
$$

3)
$$
\begin{array}{r}
425 \\
+\ 153 \\
\hline
\end{array}
$$

4)
$$
\begin{array}{r}
563 \\
+\ 125 \\
\hline
\end{array}
$$

5)
$$
\begin{array}{r}
453 \\
+\ 230 \\
\hline
\end{array}
$$

6)
$$
\begin{array}{r}
398 \\
+\ 120 \\
\hline
\end{array}
$$

7)
$$
\begin{array}{r}
689 \\
+\ 56 \\
\hline
\end{array}
$$

8)
$$
\begin{array}{r}
863 \\
+\ 325 \\
\hline
\end{array}
$$

9)
$$
\begin{array}{r}
965 \\
+\ 65 \\
\hline
\end{array}
$$

10)
$$
\begin{array}{r}
369 \\
+\ 120 \\
\hline
\end{array}
$$

11)
$$
\begin{array}{r}
187 \\
+\ 125 \\
\hline
\end{array}
$$

12)
$$
\begin{array}{r}
389 \\
+\ 150 \\
\hline
\end{array}
$$

13)
$$
\begin{array}{r}
469 \\
+\ 156 \\
\hline
\end{array}
$$

14)
$$
\begin{array}{r}
360 \\
+\ 150 \\
\hline
\end{array}
$$

15)
$$
\begin{array}{r}
689 \\
+\ 263 \\
\hline
\end{array}
$$

16)
$$
\begin{array}{r}
890 \\
+\ 345 \\
\hline
\end{array}
$$

17)
$$
\begin{array}{r}
720 \\
+\ 215 \\
\hline
\end{array}
$$

18)
$$
\begin{array}{r}
680 \\
+\ 230 \\
\hline
\end{array}
$$

Adding Hundreds

✎ **Add.**

1) $300 + 100 = ---$

2) $100 + 600 = ---$

3) $200 + 200 = ---$

4) $300 + 400 = ---$

5) $500 + 100 = ---$

6) $800 + 100 = ---$

7) $300 + 400 = ---$

8) $100 + 100 = ---$

9) $200 + 500 = ---$

10) $500 + 300 = ---$

11) $300 + 800 = ---$

12) $700 + 500 = ---$

13) $700 + 800 = ---$

14) $200 + 800 = ---$

15) $900 + 100 = ---$

16) $300 + 700 = ---$

17) $900 + 200 = ---$

18) $300 + 600 = ---$

19) $200 + 400 = ---$

20) $400 + 400 = ---$

21) $700 + 700 = ---$

22) $700 + 100 = ---$

23) $900 + 700 = ---$

24) $900 + 900 = ---$

25) If there are 700 balls in a box and Jackson puts 300 more balls inside, how many balls are in the box? _____ balls

Adding 4–Digit Numbers

✎ **Add.**

1)
$$\begin{array}{r} 2{,}135 \\ +\ 5{,}236 \\ \hline \end{array}$$

4)
$$\begin{array}{r} 3{,}125 \\ +4{,}035 \\ \hline \end{array}$$

7)
$$\begin{array}{r} 3{,}236 \\ +2{,}369 \\ \hline \end{array}$$

2)
$$\begin{array}{r} 4{,}369 \\ +\ 1{,}356 \\ \hline \end{array}$$

5)
$$\begin{array}{r} 4{,}135 \\ +2{,}194 \\ \hline \end{array}$$

8)
$$\begin{array}{r} 6{,}320 \\ +3{,}765 \\ \hline \end{array}$$

3)
$$\begin{array}{r} 6{,}598 \\ +\ 2{,}325 \\ \hline \end{array}$$

6)
$$\begin{array}{r} 5{,}036 \\ +2{,}365 \\ \hline \end{array}$$

9)
$$\begin{array}{r} 3{,}890 \\ +3{,}567 \\ \hline \end{array}$$

✎ **Find the missing numbers.**

10) $1{,}155 + \underline{\quad} = 1{,}469$

11) $400 + 3{,}000 = \underline{\quad}$

12) $5{,}200 + \underline{\quad} = 7{,}300$

13) $555 + \underline{\quad} = 1{,}886$

14) $\underline{\quad} + 920 = 1{,}550$

15) $\underline{\quad} + 2{,}670 = 4{,}230$

16) Mason sells gems. He finds a diamond in Istanbul and buys it for $3,433. Then, he flies to Cairo and purchases a bigger diamond for the bargain price of $7,922. How much does Mason spend on the two diamonds?

Subtracting 4–Digit Numbers

✎ **Subtract.**

1)
$$\begin{array}{r} 3,130 \\ -\ 1,134 \\ \hline \end{array}$$

4)
$$\begin{array}{r} 6,987 \\ -\ 6,422 \\ \hline \end{array}$$

7)
$$\begin{array}{r} 8,356 \\ -\ 5,712 \\ \hline \end{array}$$

2)
$$\begin{array}{r} 3,356 \\ -\ 2,870 \\ \hline \end{array}$$

5)
$$\begin{array}{r} 5,362 \\ -\ 3,331 \\ \hline \end{array}$$

8)
$$\begin{array}{r} 8,350 \\ -\ 2,729 \\ \hline \end{array}$$

3)
$$\begin{array}{r} 5,986 \\ -\ 2,678 \\ \hline \end{array}$$

6)
$$\begin{array}{r} 7,365 \\ -\ 2,212 \\ \hline \end{array}$$

9)
$$\begin{array}{r} 6,117 \\ -1,216 \\ \hline \end{array}$$

✎ **Find the missing number.**

10) $4,223 - \underline{\quad} = 2,320$

11) $5,856 - \underline{\quad} = 4,245$

12) $1,136 - 689 = \underline{\quad}$

13) $4,200 - \underline{\quad} = 2,450$

14) $5,870 - 2,650 = \underline{\quad}$

15) $6,360 - 4,320 = \underline{\quad}$

16) Bob had \$3,486 invested in the stock market until he lost \$2,198 on those investments. How much money does he have in the stock market now?

Estimate Sums

✎ **Estimate the sum by rounding each added to the nearest ten.**

1) $36 + 9 =$

2) $29 + 46 =$

3) $36 + 12 =$

4) $37 + 38 =$

5) $12 + 35 =$

6) $38 + 13 =$

7) $48 + 25 =$

8) $36 + 77 =$

9) $45 + 86 =$

10) $62 + 58 =$

11) $45 + 36 =$

12) $52 + 18 =$

13) $35 + 59 =$

14) $38 + 65 =$

15) $87 + 82 =$

16) $18 + 69 =$

17) $65 + 64 =$

18) $33 + 26 =$

19) $73 + 48 =$

20) $35 + 64 =$

21) $13 + 93 =$

22) $63 + 52 =$

23) $164 + 142 =$

24) $54 + 77 =$

Estimate Differences

 Estimate the difference by rounding each number to the nearest ten.

1) $58 - 23 =$

2) $34 - 24 =$

3) $75 - 48 =$

4) $43 - 24 =$

5) $69 - 46 =$

6) $42 - 23 =$

7) $77 - 47 =$

8) $49 - 28 =$

9) $94 - 48 =$

10) $79 - 59 =$

11) $68 - 26 =$

12) $83 - 37 =$

13) $73 - 43 =$

14) $58 - 42 =$

15) $82 - 52 =$

16) $65 - 43 =$

17) $99 - 81 =$

18) $42 - 24 =$

19) $58 - 47 =$

20) $89 - 28 =$

21) $81 - 65 =$

22) $68 - 14 =$

23) $76 - 6 =$

24) $78 - 31 =$

Answers of Worksheets – Chapter 2

Adding two–digit numbers

1) 68	7) 95	13) 64
2) 66	8) 65	14) 70
3) 67	9) 100	15) 98
4) 64	10) 56	16) 93
5) 85	11) 72	17) 92
6) 69	12) 57	18) 81

Subtracting two–digit numbers

1) 6	7) 47	13) 39
2) 44	8) 68	14) 23
3) 60	9) 46	15) 28
4) 17	10) 51	16) 72
5) 41	11) 43	17) 24
6) 49	12) 25	18) 33

Adding three–digit numbers

1) 562	7) 745	13) 625
2) 855	8) 1,188	14) 510
3) 578	9) 1,030	15) 952
4) 688	10) 489	16) 1,235
5) 683	11) 312	17) 935
6) 518	12) 539	18) 910

Adding hundreds

1) 400	8) 200	15) 1,000
2) 700	9) 700	16) 1,000
3) 400	10) 800	17) 1,100
4) 700	11) 1,100	18) 900
5) 600	12) 1,200	19) 600
6) 900	13) 1,500	20) 800
7) 700	14) 1,000	21) 1,400

22) 800

23) 1,600

24) 1,800

25) 1,000

Adding 4–digit numbers

1) 7,371

2) 5,725

3) 8,923

4) 7,160

5) 6,329

6) 7,401

7) 5,605

8) 10,085

9) 7,457

10) 314

11) 3,400

12) 2,100

13) 1,331

14) 630

15) 1,560

16) $11,355

Subtracting 4–digit numbers

1) 1,996

2) 486

3) 3,308

4) 565

5) 2,031

6) 5,153

7) 2,644

8) 5,621

9) 4,901

10) 1,903

11) 1,611

12) 447

13) 1,750

14) 3,220

15) 2,040

16) 1,288

Estimate sums

1) 50

2) 80

3) 50

4) 80

5) 50

6) 50

7) 80

8) 120

9) 140

10) 120

11) 90

12) 70

13) 100

14) 110

15) 170

16) 90

17) 130

18) 60

19) 120

20) 100

21) 100

22) 110

23) 300

24) 130

Estimate differences

1) 40

2) 10

3) 30

4) 20

5) 20

6) 20

7) 30

8) 20

9) 40

10) 20

11) 40

12) 40

13) 30

14) 20

15) 30

16) 30

17) 20

18) 20

19) 10

20) 60

21) 10

22) 60

23) 70

24) 50

Chapter 3: Multiplication and Division

Topics that you'll practice in this chapter:

- ✓ Multiplication

- ✓ Estimate Products

- ✓ Missing Numbers

- ✓ Division

- ✓ Long Division by One Digit

- ✓ Division with Remainders

Multiplication

✎ **Find the answers.**

1)
$$\begin{array}{r} 53 \\ \times\ 12 \\ \hline \end{array}$$

6)
$$\begin{array}{r} 45 \\ \times\ 21 \\ \hline \end{array}$$

11)
$$\begin{array}{r} 363 \\ \times\ 4 \\ \hline \end{array}$$

2)
$$\begin{array}{r} 46 \\ \times\ 10 \\ \hline \end{array}$$

7)
$$\begin{array}{r} 12 \\ \times\ 13 \\ \hline \end{array}$$

12)
$$\begin{array}{r} 36 \\ \times\ 20 \\ \hline \end{array}$$

3)
$$\begin{array}{r} 17 \\ \times\ 12 \\ \hline \end{array}$$

8)
$$\begin{array}{r} 42 \\ \times\ 20 \\ \hline \end{array}$$

13)
$$\begin{array}{r} 345 \\ \times\ 23 \\ \hline \end{array}$$

4)
$$\begin{array}{r} 45 \\ \times\ 14 \\ \hline \end{array}$$

9)
$$\begin{array}{r} 140 \\ \times\ 7 \\ \hline \end{array}$$

14)
$$\begin{array}{r} 725 \\ \times\ 30 \\ \hline \end{array}$$

5)
$$\begin{array}{r} 48 \\ \times\ 12 \\ \hline \end{array}$$

10)
$$\begin{array}{r} 564 \\ \times\ 4 \\ \hline \end{array}$$

15)
$$\begin{array}{r} 364 \\ \times\ 25 \\ \hline \end{array}$$

16) The Haunted House Ride runs 5 times a day. It has 9 cars, each of which can hold 4people. How many people can ride the Haunted House Ride in one day?

17) Each train car has 6 rows of seats. There are 7 seats in each row. How many seats are there in 8 train cars?

Estimate Products

✎ **Estimate the products.**

1) $38 \times 17 =$ 2) $13 \times 16 =$

3) $23 \times 16 =$ 4) $23 \times 12 =$

5) $65 \times 21 =$ 6) $38 \times 71 =$

7) $42 \times 92 =$ 8) $15 \times 39 =$

9) $23 \times 14 =$ 10) $73 \times 33 =$

11) $43 \times 24 =$ 12) $49 \times 13 =$

13) $58 \times 33 =$ 14) $82 \times 56 =$

15) $52 \times 77 =$ 16) $26 \times 58 =$

17) $34 \times 38 =$ 18) $33 \times 47 =$

19) $32 \times 36 =$ 20) $35 \times 47 =$

21) $75 \times 53 =$ 22) $29 \times 11 =$

23) $53 \times 11 =$ 24) $94 \times 36 =$

Missing Numbers

✎ **Find the missing numbers.**

1) $20 \times \underline{\hphantom{00}} = 80$

2) $16 \times \underline{\hphantom{00}} = 48$

3) $\underline{\hphantom{00}} \times 12 = 96$

4) $12 \times \underline{\hphantom{00}} = 48$

5) $\underline{\hphantom{00}} \times 17 = 102$

6) $15 \times \underline{\hphantom{00}} = 135$

7) $\underline{\hphantom{00}} \times 1 = 36$

8) $6 \times \underline{\hphantom{00}} = 48$

9) $80 \times \underline{\hphantom{00}} = 2,400$

10) $12 \times 7 = \underline{\hphantom{00}}$

11) $36 \times 5 = \underline{\hphantom{00}}$

12) $22 \times 4 = \underline{\hphantom{00}}$

13) $69 \times 3 = \underline{\hphantom{00}}$

14) $\underline{\hphantom{00}} \times 45 = 270$

15) $9 \times \underline{\hphantom{00}} = 360$

16) $55 \times 2 = \underline{\hphantom{00}}$

17) $70 \times \underline{\hphantom{00}} = 280$

18) $32 \times \underline{\hphantom{00}} = 256$

19) $\underline{\hphantom{00}} \times 30 = 270$

20) $25 \times 5 = \underline{\hphantom{00}}$

21) $\underline{\hphantom{00}} \times 13 = 169$

22) $19 \times \underline{\hphantom{00}} = 228$

23) $40 \times 6 = \underline{\hphantom{00}}$

24) $50 \times 3 = \underline{\hphantom{00}}$

25) $\underline{\hphantom{00}} \times 26 = 832$

26) $18 \times \underline{\hphantom{00}} = 216$

Division

✍ **Find each missing number.**

1) $16 \div \_\_ = 2$

2) $\_\_ \div 8 = 6$

3) $18 \div \_\_ = 2$

4) $\_\_ \div 5 = 9$

5) $32 \div \_\_ = 4$

6) $\_\_ \div 9 = 8$

7) $40 \div \_\_ = 5$

8) $240 \div 16 = \_\_$

9) $99 \div \_\_ = 9$

10) $80 \div 10 = \_\_$

11) $24 \div \_\_ = 3$

12) $42 \div \_\_ = 6$

13) $\_\_ \div 8 = 7$

14) $120 \div 40 = \_\_$

15) $18 \div \_\_ = 1$

16) $60 \div \_\_ = 6$

17) $\_\_ \div 14 = 9$

18) $\_\_ \div 11 = 13$

19) $70 \div \_\_ = 7$

20) $\_\_ \div 10 = 3$

21) $49 \div 7 = \_\_$

22) $100 \div 10 = \_\_$

23) $14 \div 14 = \_\_$

24) $625 \div \_\_ = 25$

25) Stella has 180 books. She wants to put them in equal numbers on 6 bookshelves. How many books can she put on a bookshelf? _____ books

26) If dividend is 144 and the quotient is 16, then what is the divisor? _____

Long Division by One Digit

✎ **Find the quotient.**

1) $5\overline{)100}$=

2) $8\overline{)64}$=

3) $13\overline{)169}$=

4) $3\overline{)24}$=

5) $12\overline{)144}$=

6) $8\overline{)48}$=

7) $2\overline{)12}$=

8) $7\overline{)21}$=

9) $9\overline{)468}$=

10) $5\overline{)30}$=

11) $4\overline{)36}$=

12) $13\overline{)65}$=

13) $8\overline{)56}$=

14) $9\overline{)90}$=

15) $8\overline{)112}$=

16) $24\overline{)360}$=

17) $2\overline{)36}$=

18) $8\overline{)24}$=

19) $4\overline{)60}$=

20) $9\overline{)153}$=

21) $6\overline{)114}$=

22) $5\overline{)90}$=

23) $10\overline{)1,170}$=

24) $11\overline{)462}$=

25) $4\overline{)540}$=

26) $8\overline{)640}$=

27) $8\overline{)216}$ =

28) $8\overline{)112}$ =

29) $15\overline{)495}$ =

30) $20\overline{)400}$ =

31) $11\overline{)484}$ =

32) $10\overline{)800}$=

33) $2\overline{)64}$=

34) $3\overline{)48}$ =

35) $4\overline{)76}$ =

36) $12\overline{)720}$=

37) $8\overline{)1,160}$=

38) $6\overline{)750}$=

39) $9\overline{)3,168}$ =

40) $4\overline{)812}$ =

41) $5\overline{)1,025}$ =

42) $3\overline{)2,589}$ =

Division with Remainders

✎ **Find the quotient with remainder.**

1) $6\overline{)38}$

2) $5\overline{)29}$

3) $8\overline{)67}$

4) $3\overline{)10}$

5) $7\overline{)53}$

6) $3\overline{)17}$

7) $12\overline{)146}$

8) $21\overline{)444}$

9) $4\overline{)22}$

10) $5\overline{)48}$

11) $10\overline{)71}$

12) $8\overline{)24}$

13) $7\overline{)51}$

14) $9\overline{)84}$

15) $6\overline{)40}$

16) $12\overline{)126}$

17) $15\overline{)228}$

18) $11\overline{)177}$

19) $13\overline{)38}$

20) $3\overline{)20}$

21) $13\overline{)222}$

22) $5\overline{)46}$

23) $4\overline{)9}$

24) $9\overline{)1450}$

25) $96\overline{)194}$

26) $36\overline{)183}$

27) $38\overline{)230}$

28) $146\overline{)443}$

29) $42\overline{)1,766}$

30) $92\overline{)554}$

31) $210\overline{)632}$

32) $135\overline{)810}$

33) $6\overline{)79}$

34) $13\overline{)161}$

35) $126\overline{)885}$

36) $85\overline{)853}$

37) $125\overline{)1502}$

38) $11\overline{)4,832}$

39) $8\overline{)2,691}$

40) $7\overline{)953}$

41) $3\overline{)2,265}$

42) $4\overline{)6,744}$

Answers of Worksheets – Chapter 3

Multiplication

1) 636	6) 945	11) 1,452	16) 180
2) 460	7) 156	12) 720	17) 336
3) 204	8) 840	13) 7,935	
4) 630	9) 980	14) 21,750	
5) 576	10) 2,256	15) 9,100	

Estimate products

1) 800	7) 3,600	13) 1,800	19) 1,200
2) 200	8) 800	14) 4,800	20) 2,000
3) 400	9) 200	15) 4,000	21) 4,000
4) 200	10) 2,100	16) 1,800	22) 3,000
5) 1,400	11) 800	17) 1,200	23) 500
6) 2,800	12) 500	18) 1,500	24) 3,600

Missing Numbers

1) 4	8) 8	15) 40	22) 12
2) 3	9) 30	16) 110	23) 240
3) 8	10) 84	17) 4	24) 150
4) 4	11) 180	18) 8	25) 32
5) 6	12) 88	19) 9	26) 12
6) 9	13) 207	20) 125	
7) 36	14) 6	21) 13	

Division

1) 8	8) 15	15) 18	22) 10
2) 48	9) 11	16) 10	23) 1
3) 9	10) 8	17) 126	24) 25
4) 45	11) 8	18) 143	25) 30
5) 8	12) 7	19) 10	26) 9
6) 72	13) 56	20) 30	
7) 8	14) 3	21) 7	

Long Division by One Digit

1) 20	12) 5	23) 117	34) 16
2) 8	13) 7	24) 42	35) 19
3) 13	14) 10	25) 135	36) 60
4) 8	15) 14	26) 80	37) 145
5) 12	16) 15	27) 27	38) 125
6) 6	17) 18	28) 14	39) 352
7) 6	18) 3	29) 33	40) 203
8) 3	19) 15	30) 20	41) 205
9) 52	20) 17	31) 44	42) 863
10) 6	21) 19	32) 80	
11) 9	22) 18	33) 32	

Division with Remainders

1) 6 R2	12) 3 R0	23) 2 R1	34) 12 R5
2) 5 R4	13) 7 R2	24) 161 R1	35) 7 R3
3) 8 R3	14) 9 R3	25) 2 R2	36) 10 R3
4) 3 R1	15) 6 R4	26) 5 R3	37) 12 R2
5) 7 R4	16) 10 R6	27) 6 R2	38) 439 R3
6) 5 R2	17) 15 R3	28) 3 R5	39) 336 R3
7) 12 R2	18) 16 R1	29) 42 R2	40) 135 R8
8) 21 R3	19) 2 R12	30) 6 R2	41) 753 R6
9) 4 R2	20) 6 R2	31) 3 R2	42) 1,685 R4
10) 9 R3	21) 17 R1	32) 6 R0	
11) 7 R1	22) 9 R1	33) 13 R1	

Chapter 4:

Patterns and Number Theory

Topics that you'll practice in this chapter:

- ✓ Repeating pattern

- ✓ Growing Patterns

- ✓ Patterns: Numbers

- ✓ Factoring Numbers

- ✓ Prime Factorization

- ✓ Greatest Common Factor

- ✓ Least Common Multiple

- ✓ Divisibility Rules

Repeating Pattern

✎ **Circle the picture that comes next in each picture pattern.**

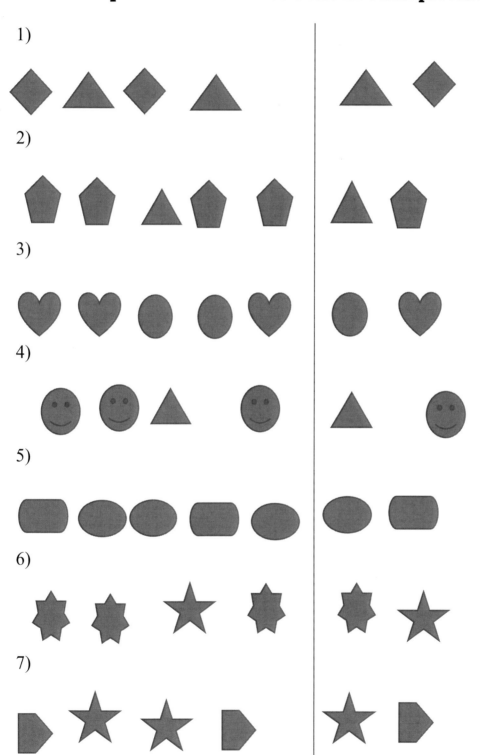

1)

2)

3)

4)

5)

6)

7)

Growing Patterns

✍ **Draw the picture that comes next in each growing pattern.**

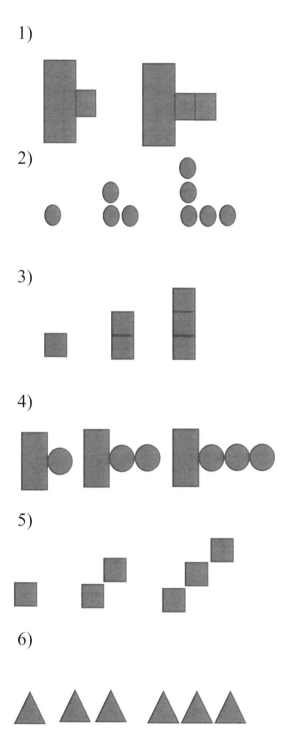

1)

2)

3)

4)

5)

6)

Patterns: Numbers

✍ **Write the numbers that come next.**

1) 11, 15, 19, 23,   ____, ____, ____, ____

2) 9, 18, 27, 36,   ____, ____, ____, ____

3) 10, 20, 30, 40,   ____, ____, ____, ____

4) 7, 14, 21, 28,   ____, ____, ____, ____

5) 10, 15, 20, 25, 30,   ____, ____, ____, ____

6) 50, 45, 40, 35, 30,   ____, ____, ____, ____

7) 14, 26, 38, 50,   ____, ____, ____, ____

✍ **Write the next three numbers in each counting sequence.**

8) −30, −22, −14, ____, ____, ____, ____

9) 525, 505, 485, ____, ____, ____, ____

10) ____, ____, 68, 78, ____, 98

11) 35, 37, ____, ____, 43, ____

12) 28, 22, ____, ____, ____

13) 62, 55, ____, ____, ____

14) 43, 40, 37, ____, ____, ____

15) 62, 44, 26, ____, ____, ____

Factoring Numbers

✍ **List all positive factors of each number.**

1) 24

9) 64

17) 44

2) 56

10) 15

18) 46

3) 42

11) 100

19) 92

4) 21

12) 80

20) 84

5) 8

13) 66

21) 54

6) 32

14) 12

22) 124

7) 36

15) 49

23) 48

8) 40

16) 81

24) 125

Prime Factorization

✎ **Factor the following numbers to their prime factors.**

1) 30	9) 81	17) 210
2) 32	10) 33	18) 120
3) 25	11) 42	19) 39
4) 21	12) 80	20) 44
5) 18	13) 75	21) 126
6) 84	14) 66	22) 50
7) 56	15) 35	23) 245
8) 15	16) 65	24) 63

Greatest Common Factor

🖎 **Find the GCF for each number pair.**

1) 6,18

2) 12,20

3) 8,24

4) 24,42

5) 20,40

6) 18,36

7) 28,56

8) 24,56

9) 20,48

10) 24,84

11) 60,72

12) 48,80

13) 24,16

14) 6,54

15) 32,64

16) 52,24

17) 16,18

18) 36,24

19) 26,40

20) 30,24

21) 12,40

22) 28,44

23) 100,60

24) 23,64

Least Common Multiple

✍ **Find the LCM for each number pair.**

1) 12, 24

2) 20, 40

3) 12, 28

4) 16, 18

5) 12, 36

6) 10, 12

7) 8, 12

8) 10, 5

9) 16, 72

10) 21, 36

11) 24, 32

12) 12, 14

13) 16, 48

14) 18, 46

15) 24, 48

16) 30, 40

17) 35, 15

18) 22, 24

19) 32, 18

20) 18, 30

21) 14, 26

22) 20, 70

23) 50, 60

24) 42, 52

Divisibility Rules

✑ **Use the divisibility rules to underline the factors of the number.**

1) 15   2 <u>3</u> 4 <u>5</u> 6 7 8 9 10

2) 24   2 3 4 5 6 7 8 9 10

3) 18   2 3 4 5 6 7 8 9 10

4) 30   2 3 4 5 6 7 8 9 10

5) 32   2 3 4 5 6 7 8 9 10

6) 10   2 3 4 5 6 7 8 9 10

7) 64   2 3 4 5 6 7 8 9 10

8) 45   2 3 4 5 6 7 8 9 10

9) 82   2 3 4 5 6 7 8 9 10

10) 66   2 3 4 5 6 7 8 9 10

11) 144   2 3 4 5 6 7 8 9 10

12) 124   2 3 4 5 6 7 8 9 10

                2 3 4 5 6 7 8 9 10
13) 35

Answers of Worksheets – Chapter 4

Repeating pattern

1)

2)

3)

4)

5)

6)

7)

Growing patterns

1)

2)

3)

4)

5)

6)

Patterns: Numbers

1) 11, 15, 19, 23, 27, 31, 35, 39

2) 9, 18, 27, 36, 45, 54, 63, 72

3) 10, 20, 30, 40, 50, 60, 70, 80

4) 7, 14, 21, 28, 35, 42, 49, 56

5) 10, 15, 20, 25, 30, 35, 40, 45

6) 50, 45, 40, 35, 30, 25, 20, 15

7) 14, 26, 38, 50, 62, 74, 86, 98

8) $-6, -2, 10, 18$

9) $465, 445, 425$

10) $48- 58- 68- 78- 88- 98$

11) $35- 37- 39- 41- 43- 45$

12) $16- 10 - 4$

13) $48- 41- 34$

14) $34, 31, 28$

15) $8, -10, - 28$

Factoring Numbers

1) $1, 2, 3, 4, 6, 8, 12, 24$

2) $1, 2, 4, 7, 8, 14, 28, 56$

3) $1, 2, 3, 6, 7, 14, 21, 42$

4) $1, 3, 7, 21$

5) $1, 2, 4, 8$

6) $1, 2, 4, 8, 16, 32$

7) $1, 2, 3, 4, 6, 9, 12, 18, 36$

8) $1, 2, 4, 5, 8, 10, 20, 40$

9) $1, 2, 4, 8, 16, 32, 64$

10) $1, 3, 5, 15$

11) $1, 2, 4, 5, 10, 20, 25, 50, 100$

12) $1, 2, 4, 5, 8, 10, 16, 20, 40, 80$

13) $1, 2, 3, 6, 11, 22, 33, 66$

14) $1, 2, 3, 4, 6, 12$

15) $1, 7, 49$

16) $1, 3, 9, 27, 81$

17) $1, 2, 4, 11, 22, 44$

18) $1, 2, 23, 46$

19) $1, 2, 4, 23, 46, 92$

20) $1, 2, 3, 4, 6, 7, 12, 14, 21, 28, 42, 84$

21) $1, 2, 3, 6, 9, 18, 27, 54$

22) $1, 2, 4, 31, 62, 124$

23) $1, 2, 3, 4, 6, 8, 12, 16, 24, 48$

24) $1, 5, 25, 125$

Prime Factorization

1) $2 . 3 . 5$

2) $2 . 2 . 2 . 2 . 2$

3) $5 . 5$

4) $3 . 7$

5) $3 . 2 . 3$

6) $2 . 2 . 3 . 7$

7) $2 . 2 . 2 . 7$

8) $5 . 3$

9) $3 . 3 . 3 . 3$

10) $3 . 11$

11) $2 . 3 . 7$

12) $2 . 2 . 2 . 2 . 5$

13) $3 . 5 . 5$

14) $3 . 2 . 11$

15) $5 . 7$

16) $5 . 13$

17) $2 . 7 . 3 . 5$

18) $2 . 2 . 2 . 5 . 3$

19) $3 . 13$

20) $2 . 2 . 11$

21) $3 . 3 . 2 . 7$

22) $2 . 5 . 5$

23) $7 . 7 . 5$

24) $3 . 3 . 7$

Greatest Common Factor

1) 6

2) 4

3) 8

4) 6

5) 20

6) 18

7) 14

8) 4

9) 4

10) 12

11) 12

12) 16

13) 8   17) 2   21) 4

14) 6   18) 12   22) 4

15) 32   19) 1   23) 20

16) 4   20) 6   24) 1

Least Common Multiple

1) 24   9) 144   17) 105

2) 40   10) 252   18) 264

3) 84   11) 96   19) 288

4) 144   12) 84   20) 90

5) 36   13) 48   21) 182

6) 60   14) 414   22) 140

7) 24   15) 48   23) 300

8) 10   16) 120   24) 1,092

Divisibility Rules

1) 15 — 2 <u>3</u> 4 <u>5</u> 6 7 8 9 10

2) 24 — <u>2</u> 3 <u>4</u> 5 <u>6</u> 7 <u>8</u> 9 10

3) 18 — <u>2</u> <u>3</u> 4 5 <u>6</u> 7 8 <u>9</u> 10

4) 30 — <u>2</u> <u>3</u> 4 <u>5</u> <u>6</u> 7 8 9 <u>10</u>

5) 32 — <u>2</u> 3 <u>4</u> 5 6 7 <u>8</u> 9 10

6) 10 — <u>2</u> 3 4 <u>5</u> 6 7 8 9 <u>10</u>

7) 64 — <u>2</u> 3 <u>4</u> 5 6 7 <u>8</u> 9 10

8) 45 — 2 <u>3</u> 4 <u>5</u> 6 7 8 <u>9</u> 10

9) 82 — <u>2</u> 3 4 5 6 7 8 9 10

10) 66 — <u>2</u> <u>3</u> 4 5 <u>6</u> 7 8 9 10

11) 144 — <u>2</u> 3 4 5 <u>6</u> 7 <u>8</u> <u>9</u> 10

12) 124 — <u>2</u> 3 <u>4</u> 5 6 7 8 9 10

13) 35 — 2 *3* 4 <u>5</u> 6 <u>7</u> 8 9 10

Chapter 5:

Fractions

Topics that you'll practice in this chapter:

✓ Fractions

✓ Add Fractions with Like Denominators

✓ Subtract Fractions with Like Denominators

✓ Compare Sums and Differences of Fractions with Like Denominators

✓ Add 3 or More Fractions with Like Denominators

✓ Simplifying Fractions

✓ Add Fractions with Unlike Denominators

✓ Subtract Fractions with Unlike Denominators

✓ Add and Subtract Fractions with Denominators of 10 and 100

Add Fractions with Like Denominators

✎ **Add fractions.**

1) $\dfrac{3}{4} + \dfrac{1}{4} =$

2) $\dfrac{3}{7} + \dfrac{4}{7} =$

3) $\dfrac{5}{7} + \dfrac{4}{7} =$

4) $\dfrac{5}{2} + \dfrac{5}{2} =$

5) $\dfrac{4}{11} + \dfrac{3}{11} =$

6) $\dfrac{3}{8} + \dfrac{4}{8} =$

7) $\dfrac{7}{5} + \dfrac{4}{5} =$

8) $\dfrac{5}{13} + \dfrac{6}{13} =$

9) $\dfrac{5}{17} + \dfrac{10}{17} =$

10) $\dfrac{3}{9} + \dfrac{5}{9} =$

11) $\dfrac{5}{14} + \dfrac{6}{14} =$

12) $\dfrac{6}{23} + \dfrac{10}{23} =$

13) $\dfrac{8}{15} + \dfrac{7}{15} =$

14) $\dfrac{4}{17} + \dfrac{3}{17} =$

15) $\dfrac{7}{15} + \dfrac{3}{15} =$

16) $\dfrac{15}{38} + \dfrac{12}{38} =$

17) $\dfrac{7}{19} + \dfrac{10}{19} =$

18) $\dfrac{6}{22} + \dfrac{8}{22} =$

19) $\dfrac{20}{41} + \dfrac{11}{41} =$

20) $\dfrac{8}{39} + \dfrac{15}{39} =$

21) $\dfrac{20}{71} + \dfrac{16}{71} =$

22) $\dfrac{32}{55} + \dfrac{10}{55} =$

Subtract Fractions with Like Denominators

✑ **Subtract fractions.**

1) $\dfrac{3}{8} - \dfrac{2}{8} =$

2) $\dfrac{2}{9} - \dfrac{1}{9} =$

3) $\dfrac{14}{18} - \dfrac{8}{18} =$

4) $\dfrac{7}{6} - \dfrac{3}{6} =$

5) $\dfrac{4}{15} - \dfrac{3}{15} =$

6) $\dfrac{5}{21} - \dfrac{3}{21} =$

7) $\dfrac{7}{8} - \dfrac{5}{8} =$

8) $\dfrac{11}{42} - \dfrac{7}{42} =$

9) $\dfrac{20}{18} - \dfrac{7}{18} =$

10) $\dfrac{7}{24} - \dfrac{6}{24} =$

11) $\dfrac{15}{33} - \dfrac{12}{33} =$

12) $\dfrac{10}{63} - \dfrac{9}{63} =$

13) $\dfrac{9}{27} - \dfrac{6}{27} =$

14) $\dfrac{35}{40} - \dfrac{17}{40} =$

15) $\dfrac{22}{20} - \dfrac{9}{20} =$

16) $\dfrac{26}{40} - \dfrac{18}{40} =$

17) $\dfrac{32}{23} - \dfrac{28}{23} =$

18) $\dfrac{16}{82} - \dfrac{6}{82} =$

19) $\dfrac{35}{40} - \dfrac{15}{40} =$

20) $\dfrac{29}{35} - \dfrac{19}{35} =$

21) $\dfrac{21}{70} - \dfrac{11}{70} =$

22) $\dfrac{9}{29} - \dfrac{8}{29} =$

Add and Subtract Fractions with Like Denominators

✍ **Add fractions.**

1) $\dfrac{1}{4} + \dfrac{3}{4} =$

6) $\dfrac{4}{25} + \dfrac{1}{25} =$

2) $\dfrac{1}{7} + \dfrac{6}{7} =$

7) $\dfrac{3}{17} + \dfrac{2}{17} =$

3) $\dfrac{4}{9} + \dfrac{2}{9} =$

8) $\dfrac{4}{6} + \dfrac{2}{6} =$

4) $\dfrac{5}{9} + \dfrac{2}{9} =$

9) $\dfrac{1}{12} + \dfrac{1}{12} =$

5) $\dfrac{3}{15} + \dfrac{8}{15} =$

10) $\dfrac{16}{23} + \dfrac{5}{23} =$

✍ **Subtract fractions.**

11) $\dfrac{4}{9} - \dfrac{2}{9} =$

16) $\dfrac{3}{14} - \dfrac{1}{14} =$

12) $\dfrac{6}{11} - \dfrac{5}{11} =$

17) $\dfrac{15}{55} - \dfrac{13}{55} =$

13) $\dfrac{3}{18} - \dfrac{2}{18} =$

18) $\dfrac{25}{75} - \dfrac{23}{75} =$

14) $\dfrac{10}{19} - \dfrac{3}{19} =$

19) $\dfrac{19}{67} - \dfrac{17}{67} =$

15) $\dfrac{9}{21} - \dfrac{4}{21} =$

20) $\dfrac{12}{85} - \dfrac{7}{85} =$

Compare Sums and Differences of Fractions with Like Denominators

✎ **Evaluate and compare. Write < or > or =.**

1) $\dfrac{1}{6} + \dfrac{5}{6} \; \square \; \dfrac{1}{6}$

2) $\dfrac{1}{7} + \dfrac{6}{7} \; \square \; 1$

3) $\dfrac{1}{7} + \dfrac{1}{7} \; \square \; \dfrac{2}{7}$

4) $\dfrac{1}{5} + \dfrac{2}{5} \; \square \; \dfrac{1}{5}$

5) $\dfrac{3}{9} + \dfrac{6}{9} \; \square \; \dfrac{1}{2}$

6) $\dfrac{7}{8} - \dfrac{3}{8} \; \square \; \dfrac{6}{8}$

7) $\dfrac{7}{15} + \dfrac{2}{15} \; \square \; \dfrac{7}{15}$

8) $\dfrac{7}{11} - \dfrac{5}{11} \; \square \; \dfrac{9}{11}$

9) $\dfrac{10}{19} - \dfrac{6}{19} \; \square \; \dfrac{3}{19}$

10) $\dfrac{3}{9} + \dfrac{1}{9} \; \square \; \dfrac{1}{9}$

11) $\dfrac{10}{12} + \dfrac{1}{12} \; \square \; \dfrac{9}{12}$

12) $\dfrac{17}{16} - \dfrac{3}{16} \; \square \; \dfrac{17}{16}$

13) $\dfrac{11}{17} + \dfrac{6}{17} \; \square \; \dfrac{18}{17}$

14) $\dfrac{15}{13} - \dfrac{5}{13} \; \square \; \dfrac{12}{13}$

15) $\dfrac{28}{32} - \dfrac{15}{32} \; \square \; \dfrac{25}{32}$

16) $\dfrac{25}{40} + \dfrac{15}{40} \; \square \; \dfrac{17}{40}$

17) $\dfrac{25}{85} - \dfrac{3}{85} \; \square \; \dfrac{9}{85}$

18) $\dfrac{35}{71} - \dfrac{20}{71} \; \square \; \dfrac{30}{71}$

19) $\dfrac{2}{18} + \dfrac{5}{18} \; \square \; \dfrac{5}{18}$

20) $\dfrac{18}{47} + \dfrac{13}{47} \; \square \; \dfrac{30}{47}$

Add 3 or More Fractions with Like Denominators

✎ **Add fractions.**

1) $\dfrac{1}{7} + \dfrac{1}{7} + \dfrac{5}{7} =$

2) $\dfrac{1}{5} + \dfrac{1}{5} + \dfrac{1}{5} =$

3) $\dfrac{1}{10} + \dfrac{3}{10} + \dfrac{2}{10} =$

4) $\dfrac{6}{14} + \dfrac{7}{14} + \dfrac{1}{14} =$

5) $\dfrac{2}{5} + \dfrac{2}{5} + \dfrac{1}{5} =$

6) $\dfrac{4}{13} + \dfrac{5}{13} + \dfrac{1}{13} =$

7) $\dfrac{1}{6} + \dfrac{1}{6} + \dfrac{1}{6} =$

8) $\dfrac{6}{19} + \dfrac{5}{19} + \dfrac{4}{19} =$

9) $\dfrac{3}{21} + \dfrac{2}{21} + \dfrac{3}{21} =$

10) $\dfrac{4}{32} + \dfrac{2}{32} + \dfrac{1}{32} =$

11) $\dfrac{3}{28} + \dfrac{7}{28} + \dfrac{4}{28} =$

12) $\dfrac{7}{31} + \dfrac{15}{31} + \dfrac{4}{31} =$

13) $\dfrac{8}{40} + \dfrac{4}{40} + \dfrac{3}{40} =$

14) $\dfrac{2}{19} + \dfrac{3}{19} + \dfrac{7}{19} =$

15) $\dfrac{5}{52} + \dfrac{5}{52} + \dfrac{5}{52} =$

16) $\dfrac{13}{60} + \dfrac{9}{60} + \dfrac{12}{60} =$

17) $\dfrac{8}{19} + \dfrac{5}{19} + \dfrac{5}{19} =$

18) $\dfrac{3}{41} + \dfrac{5}{41} + \dfrac{6}{41} =$

19) $\dfrac{9}{48} + \dfrac{3}{48} + \dfrac{7}{48} =$

20) $\dfrac{7}{61} + \dfrac{15}{61} + \dfrac{14}{61} =$

21) $\dfrac{17}{53} + \dfrac{12}{53} + \dfrac{5}{53} =$

22) $\dfrac{22}{80} + \dfrac{15}{80} + \dfrac{13}{80} =$

Simplifying Fractions

✎ **Simplify each fraction to its lowest terms.**

1) $\dfrac{14}{28} =$

2) $\dfrac{16}{56} =$

3) $\dfrac{15}{20} =$

4) $\dfrac{30}{120} =$

5) $\dfrac{54}{144} =$

6) $\dfrac{91}{42} =$

7) $\dfrac{11}{44} =$

8) $\dfrac{9}{18} =$

9) $\dfrac{130}{260} =$

10) $\dfrac{63}{441} =$

11) $\dfrac{26}{78} =$

12) $\dfrac{45}{60} =$

13) $\dfrac{225}{275} =$

14) $\dfrac{27}{30} =$

15) $\dfrac{240}{720} =$

16) $\dfrac{315}{882} =$

17) $\dfrac{38}{95} =$

18) $\dfrac{138}{207} =$

19) $\dfrac{105}{240} =$

20) $\dfrac{195}{260} =$

21) $\dfrac{204}{255} =$

✎ **Solve each problem.**

22) Which of the following fractions equal to $\dfrac{7}{6}$? _____

    A. $\dfrac{24}{72}$ B. $\dfrac{238}{204}$ C. $\dfrac{106}{65}$ D. $\dfrac{145}{88}$

23) Which of the following fractions equal to $\dfrac{2}{7}$? _____

    A. $\dfrac{58}{203}$ B. $\dfrac{32}{287}$ C. $\dfrac{36}{260}$ D. $\dfrac{39}{98}$

24) Which of the following fractions equal to $\dfrac{2}{9}$? _____

    A. $\dfrac{84}{386}$ B. $\dfrac{120}{540}$ C. $\dfrac{40}{108}$ D. $\dfrac{109}{525}$

Add and Subtract Fractions with Unlike

Denominators

✎ Find the sum.

1) $\frac{2}{7} + \frac{5}{7} =$

2) $\frac{1}{4} + \frac{1}{3} =$

3) $\frac{3}{8} + \frac{1}{2} =$

4) $\frac{4}{5} + \frac{7}{3} =$

5) $\frac{5}{3} + \frac{7}{8} =$

6) $\frac{7}{12} + \frac{1}{13} =$

7) $\frac{5}{14} + \frac{1}{6} =$

8) $\frac{4}{6} + \frac{3}{8} =$

9) $\frac{5}{12} + \frac{3}{8} =$

10) $\frac{3}{9} + \frac{1}{2} =$

11) $\frac{3}{7} + \frac{1}{5} =$

12) $\frac{3}{12} + \frac{5}{4} =$

✎ Find the difference.

13) $\frac{1}{4} - \frac{1}{6} =$

14) $\frac{3}{5} - \frac{1}{7} =$

15) $\frac{2}{5} - \frac{1}{6} =$

16) $\frac{3}{7} - \frac{1}{3} =$

17) $\frac{7}{9} - \frac{2}{5} =$

18) $\frac{4}{3} - \frac{1}{5} =$

19) $\frac{2}{3} - \frac{1}{7} =$

20) $\frac{5}{4} - \frac{2}{7} =$

21) $\frac{4}{12} - \frac{1}{10} =$

22) $\frac{7}{20} - \frac{1}{10} =$

23) $\frac{7}{16} - \frac{1}{12} =$

24) $\frac{7}{8} - \frac{3}{32} =$

25) $\frac{5}{8} - \frac{3}{7} =$

26) $\frac{5}{27} - \frac{1}{9} =$

27) $\frac{2}{15} - \frac{1}{12} =$

28) $\frac{3}{12} - \frac{2}{18} =$

29) $\frac{4}{21} - \frac{3}{16} =$

30) $\frac{5}{8} - \frac{3}{33} =$

Add Fractions with Denominators of 10 and 100

✎ **Add fractions.**

1) $\dfrac{7}{10} + \dfrac{50}{100} =$

2) $\dfrac{3}{10} + \dfrac{22}{100} =$

3) $\dfrac{22}{100} + \dfrac{7}{10} =$

4) $\dfrac{63}{100} + \dfrac{1}{10} =$

5) $\dfrac{78}{100} + \dfrac{3}{10} =$

6) $\dfrac{4}{10} + \dfrac{40}{100} =$

7) $\dfrac{40}{100} + \dfrac{1}{10} =$

8) $\dfrac{30}{100} + \dfrac{8}{10} =$

9) $\dfrac{55}{100} + \dfrac{12}{10} =$

10) $\dfrac{8}{10} + \dfrac{15}{100} =$

11) $\dfrac{5}{10} + \dfrac{20}{100} =$

12) $\dfrac{60}{100} + \dfrac{3}{10} =$

13) $\dfrac{36}{100} + \dfrac{12}{10} =$

14) $\dfrac{34}{100} + \dfrac{6}{10} =$

15) $\dfrac{25}{100} + \dfrac{11}{10} =$

16) $\dfrac{1}{10} + \dfrac{82}{100} =$

17) $\dfrac{21}{100} + \dfrac{4}{10} =$

18) $\dfrac{26}{100} + \dfrac{9}{10} =$

19) $\dfrac{52}{100} + \dfrac{7}{10} =$

20) $\dfrac{7}{10} + \dfrac{40}{100} =$

21) $\dfrac{32}{100} + \dfrac{7}{10} =$

22) $\dfrac{41}{100} + \dfrac{1}{10} =$

Add and Subtract Fractions with Denominators of 10, 100, and 1000

✍ **Evaluate fractions.**

1) $\dfrac{22}{100} - \dfrac{3}{10} =$

2) $\dfrac{42}{100} - \dfrac{7}{10} =$

3) $\dfrac{8}{10} - \dfrac{25}{100} =$

4) $\dfrac{3}{10} + \dfrac{27}{100} =$

5) $\dfrac{15}{100} + \dfrac{350}{1000} =$

6) $\dfrac{83}{100} - \dfrac{420}{1000} =$

7) $\dfrac{35}{100} + \dfrac{650}{1000} =$

8) $\dfrac{3}{10} + \dfrac{160}{1000} =$

9) $\dfrac{20}{100} - \dfrac{450}{1000} =$

10) $\dfrac{97}{100} - \dfrac{5}{10} =$

11) $\dfrac{650}{1000} + \dfrac{13}{10} =$

12) $\dfrac{62}{100} + \dfrac{440}{1000} =$

13) $\dfrac{9}{10} - \dfrac{15}{100} =$

14) $\dfrac{75}{100} - \dfrac{5}{10} =$

15) $\dfrac{80}{100} - \dfrac{9}{10} =$

16) $\dfrac{950}{1000} - \dfrac{9}{100} =$

17) $\dfrac{300}{1000} + \dfrac{11}{100} =$

18) $\dfrac{520}{1000} - \dfrac{12}{10} =$

19) $\dfrac{70}{100} - \dfrac{11}{10} =$

20) $\dfrac{30}{100} - \dfrac{210}{1000} =$

Answers of Worksheets – Chapter 5

Add Fractions with Like Denominators

1) 1

2) 1

3) $\frac{9}{7}$

4) 5

5) $\frac{7}{11}$

6) $\frac{7}{8}$

7) $\frac{11}{5}$

8) $\frac{11}{13}$

9) $\frac{15}{17}$

10) $\frac{8}{9}$

11) $\frac{11}{14}$

12) $\frac{16}{23}$

13) 1

14) $\frac{7}{17}$

15) $\frac{10}{15}$

16) $\frac{27}{38}$

17) $\frac{17}{19}$

18) $\frac{14}{22}$

19) $\frac{31}{41}$

20) $\frac{23}{39}$

21) $\frac{36}{71}$

22) $\frac{42}{55}$

Subtract Fractions with Like Denominators

1) $\frac{1}{8}$

2) $\frac{1}{9}$

3) $\frac{1}{3}$

4) $\frac{2}{3}$

5) $\frac{1}{15}$

6) $\frac{2}{21}$

7) $\frac{1}{4}$

8) $\frac{4}{42}$

9) $\frac{13}{18}$

10) $\frac{1}{24}$

11) $\frac{1}{11}$

12) $\frac{1}{63}$

13) $\frac{1}{9}$

14) $\frac{9}{20}$

15) $\frac{13}{20}$

16) $\frac{1}{5}$

17) $\frac{4}{23}$

18) $\frac{5}{41}$

19) $\frac{1}{2}$

20) $\frac{2}{7}$

21) $\frac{1}{7}$

22) $\frac{1}{29}$

Add and Subtract Fractions with Like Denominators

1) 1

2) 1

3) $\frac{2}{3}$

4) $\frac{7}{9}$

5) $\frac{11}{15}$

6) $\frac{1}{5}$

7) $\frac{5}{17}$

8) 1

9) $\frac{1}{6}$

10) $\frac{21}{23}$

11) $\frac{2}{9}$

12) $\frac{1}{11}$

13) $\frac{1}{18}$

14) $\frac{7}{19}$

15) $\frac{5}{21}$

16) $\frac{1}{7}$

17) $\frac{2}{55}$

18) $\frac{2}{75}$

19) $\frac{2}{67}$

20) $\frac{5}{85}$

Compare Sums and Differences of Fractions with Like Denominators

1) $1 > \frac{1}{6}$

2) $1 = 1$

3) $\frac{2}{7} = \frac{2}{7}$

4) $\frac{3}{5} > \frac{1}{5}$

5) $1 > \frac{1}{2}$

6) $\frac{4}{8} < \frac{6}{8}$

7) $\frac{9}{15} > \frac{7}{15}$

8) $\frac{2}{11} < \frac{9}{11}$

9) $\frac{4}{19} > \frac{3}{19}$

10) $\frac{4}{9} > \frac{1}{9}$

11) $\frac{11}{12} > \frac{9}{12}$

12) $\frac{14}{16} < \frac{17}{16}$

13) $1 > \frac{18}{21}$

14) $\frac{10}{13} < \frac{12}{13}$

15) $\frac{13}{32} < \frac{25}{32}$

16) $1 > \frac{17}{40}$

17) $\frac{22}{85} > \frac{9}{85}$

18) $\frac{15}{71} < \frac{30}{71}$

19) $\frac{7}{18} > \frac{5}{18}$

20) $\frac{31}{47} > \frac{30}{47}$

Add 3 or More Fractions with Like Denominators

1) 1

2) $\frac{3}{5}$

3) $\frac{3}{5}$

4) 1

5) 1

6) $\frac{10}{13}$

7) $\frac{1}{2}$

8) $\frac{15}{19}$

9) $\frac{8}{21}$

10) $\frac{7}{32}$

11) $\frac{1}{2}$

12) $\frac{26}{31}$

13) $\frac{15}{40}$

14) $\frac{12}{19}$

15) $\frac{15}{52}$

16) $\frac{34}{60}$

17) $\frac{18}{19}$

18) $\frac{14}{41}$

19) $\frac{19}{48}$

20) $\frac{36}{61}$

21) $\frac{34}{53}$

22) $\frac{50}{80}$

Simplifying Fractions

1) $\frac{1}{2}$

2) $\frac{2}{7}$

3) $\frac{3}{4}$

4) $\frac{1}{4}$

5) $\frac{3}{8}$

6) $\frac{13}{6}$

7) $\frac{1}{4}$

8) $\frac{1}{2}$

9) $\frac{1}{2}$

10) $\frac{1}{7}$

11) $\frac{1}{3}$

12) $\frac{3}{4}$

13) $\frac{9}{11}$

14) $\frac{9}{10}$

15) $\frac{1}{3}$

16) $\frac{5}{14}$

17) $\frac{2}{5}$

18) $\frac{2}{3}$

19) $\frac{7}{16}$

20) $\frac{3}{4}$

21) $\frac{4}{5}$

22) B

23) A

24) B

Add and Subtract fractions with unlike denominators

1) $\frac{7}{7} = 1$ 9) $\frac{19}{24}$ 17) $\frac{17}{45}$ 25) $\frac{11}{56}$

2) $\frac{7}{12}$ 10) $\frac{5}{6}$ 18) $\frac{17}{15}$ 26) $\frac{2}{27}$

3) $\frac{7}{8}$ 11) $\frac{22}{35}$ 19) $\frac{11}{21}$ 27) $\frac{1}{20}$

4) $\frac{47}{15}$ 12) $\frac{3}{2}$ 20) $\frac{27}{28}$ 28) $\frac{5}{36}$

5) $\frac{61}{24}$ 13) $\frac{1}{12}$ 21) $\frac{7}{30}$ 29) $\frac{1}{336}$

6) $\frac{103}{156}$ 14) $\frac{16}{35}$ 22) $\frac{1}{4}$ 30) $\frac{47}{88}$

7) $\frac{11}{21}$ 15) $\frac{7}{30}$ 23) $\frac{17}{48}$

8) $\frac{25}{24}$ 16) $\frac{2}{21}$ 24) $\frac{25}{32}$

Add fractions with denominators of 10 and 100

1) $\frac{6}{5}$ 7) $\frac{1}{2}$ 13) $\frac{39}{25}$ 19) $\frac{61}{50}$

2) $\frac{13}{25}$ 8) $\frac{11}{10}$ 14) $\frac{47}{50}$ 20) $\frac{11}{10}$

3) $\frac{23}{25}$ 9) $\frac{7}{4}$ 15) $\frac{27}{20}$ 21) $\frac{51}{50}$

4) $\frac{73}{100}$ 10) $\frac{19}{20}$ 16) $\frac{23}{25}$ 22) $\frac{51}{100}$

5) $\frac{27}{25}$ 11) $\frac{7}{10}$ 17) $\frac{61}{100}$

6) $\frac{4}{5}$ 12) $\frac{9}{10}$ 18) $\frac{29}{25}$

Add and subtract fractions with denominators of 10, 100, and 1000

1) $-\frac{2}{25}$ 6) $\frac{41}{100}$ 11) $\frac{39}{20}$ 16) $\frac{43}{50}$

2) $-\frac{7}{25}$ 7) 1 12) $\frac{53}{50}$ 17) $\frac{41}{100}$

3) $\frac{11}{20}$ 8) $\frac{23}{50}$ 13) $\frac{3}{4}$ 18) $-\frac{17}{25}$

4) $\frac{57}{100}$ 9) $-\frac{1}{4}$ 14) $\frac{1}{4}$ 19) $-\frac{2}{5}$

5) $\frac{1}{2}$ 10) $\frac{47}{100}$ 15) $-\frac{1}{10}$ 20) $\frac{9}{100}$

Chapter 6:

Mixed Numbers

Topics that you'll practice in this chapter:

- ✓ Fractions to Mixed Numbers

- ✓ Mixed Numbers to Fractions

- ✓ Add and Subtract Mixed Numbers

- ✓ Multiplying and Dividing Mixed Numbers

Fractions to Mixed Numbers

✎ **Convert fractions to mixed numbers.**

1) $\dfrac{10}{3} =$

2) $\dfrac{13}{2} =$

3) $\dfrac{23}{3} =$

4) $\dfrac{11}{2} =$

5) $\dfrac{23}{5} =$

6) $\dfrac{19}{3} =$

7) $\dfrac{21}{4} =$

8) $\dfrac{32}{5} =$

9) $\dfrac{13}{9} =$

10) $\dfrac{18}{7} =$

11) $\dfrac{44}{7} =$

12) $\dfrac{32}{6} =$

13) $\dfrac{19}{5} =$

14) $\dfrac{28}{5} =$

15) $\dfrac{15}{2} =$

16) $\dfrac{81}{10} =$

17) $\dfrac{25}{2} =$

18) $\dfrac{24}{10} =$

19) $\dfrac{14}{3} =$

20) $\dfrac{34}{5} =$

21) $\dfrac{29}{5} =$

22) $\dfrac{87}{10} =$

23) $\dfrac{17}{3} =$

24) $\dfrac{65}{8} =$

25) $\dfrac{13}{2} =$

26) $\dfrac{19}{4} =$

27) $\dfrac{36}{5} =$

28) $\dfrac{22}{3} =$

29) $\dfrac{45}{8} =$

30) $\dfrac{17}{5} =$

Mixed Numbers to Fractions

✎ **Convert to fraction.**

1) $4\frac{1}{2} =$

2) $2\frac{2}{3} =$

3) $1\frac{2}{3} =$

4) $2\frac{1}{5} =$

5) $8\frac{2}{5} =$

6) $3\frac{1}{2} =$

7) $6\frac{5}{3} =$

8) $1\frac{2}{5} =$

9) $5\frac{2}{7} =$

10) $3\frac{2}{4} =$

11) $3\frac{2}{8} =$

12) $5\frac{1}{3} =$

13) $3\frac{5}{7} =$

14) $2\frac{3}{4} =$

15) $8\frac{5}{7} =$

16) $5\frac{5}{9} =$

17) $8\frac{9}{10} =$

18) $6\frac{5}{6} =$

19) $7\frac{2}{7} =$

20) $3\frac{9}{10} =$

21) $3\frac{2}{5} =$

22) $3\frac{4}{5} =$

23) $2\frac{1}{11} =$

24) $2\frac{1}{4} =$

25) $2\frac{4}{8} =$

26) $6\frac{2}{7} =$

27) $4\frac{3}{4} =$

28) $10\frac{6}{7} =$

29) $10\frac{7}{9} =$

30) $1\frac{1}{5} =$

31) $5\frac{6}{10} =$

32) $11\frac{1}{22} =$

33) $3\frac{15}{20} =$

Add and Subtract Mixed Numbers

✎ Find the sum.

1) $4\frac{1}{3} + 1\frac{1}{6} =$

2) $4\frac{1}{2} + 2\frac{1}{2} =$

3) $2\frac{3}{7} + 3\frac{1}{7} =$

4) $3\frac{1}{6} + 1\frac{1}{6} =$

5) $1\frac{3}{8} + 1\frac{5}{32} =$

6) $2\frac{5}{16} + 3\frac{3}{4} =$

7) $7\frac{1}{8} + 2\frac{3}{4} =$

8) $3\frac{7}{9} + 3\frac{1}{4} =$

9) $4\frac{3}{5} + 2\frac{6}{10} =$

10) $10\frac{5}{15} + 3\frac{3}{20} =$

✎ Find the difference.

11) $2\frac{1}{4} - 1\frac{1}{4} =$

12) $4\frac{1}{2} - 3\frac{1}{2} =$

13) $5\frac{1}{2} - 2\frac{1}{4} =$

14) $6\frac{1}{6} - 5\frac{1}{3} =$

15) $7\frac{1}{2} - 1\frac{1}{10} =$

16) $6\frac{1}{2} - 2\frac{1}{4} =$

17) $4\frac{1}{5} - 3\frac{1}{7} =$

18) $15\frac{3}{25} - 12\frac{1}{5} =$

19) $12\frac{2}{3} - 5\frac{5}{8} =$

20) $15\frac{3}{4} - 10\frac{2}{3} =$

21) $3\frac{1}{2} - 2\frac{1}{5} =$

22) $3\frac{1}{8} - 2\frac{1}{14} =$

23) $12\frac{2}{8} - 10\frac{2}{4} =$

24) $11\frac{1}{9} - 3\frac{1}{21} =$

25) $11\frac{3}{8} - 8\frac{1}{9} =$

26) $13\frac{2}{8} - 7\frac{2}{24} =$

Multiplying and Dividing Mixed Numbers

✎ Find the product.

1) $6\frac{1}{2} \times 3\frac{1}{8} =$

2) $2\frac{1}{2} \times 3\frac{1}{2} =$

3) $3\frac{2}{3} \times 3\frac{1}{4} =$

4) $5\frac{1}{2} \times 3\frac{2}{7} =$

5) $3\frac{4}{11} \times 3\frac{3}{11} =$

6) $3\frac{2}{3} \times 10\frac{2}{7} =$

7) $2\frac{3}{5} \times 3\frac{3}{4} =$

8) $2\frac{4}{6} \times 3\frac{2}{8} =$

9) $3\frac{2}{4} \times 2\frac{3}{4} =$

10) $3\frac{5}{9} \times 3\frac{5}{7} =$

✎ Find the quotient.

11) $1\frac{2}{5} \div 3\frac{1}{5} =$

12) $4\frac{1}{4} \div 2\frac{1}{2} =$

13) $10\frac{1}{2} \div 1\frac{2}{3} =$

14) $10\frac{1}{6} \div 8\frac{3}{5} =$

15) $3\frac{1}{18} \div 2\frac{1}{6} =$

16) $3\frac{1}{10} \div 2\frac{3}{5} =$

17) $1\frac{4}{12} \div 1\frac{1}{8} =$

18) $6\frac{1}{5} \div 6\frac{2}{4} =$

19) $7\frac{3}{4} \div 6\frac{2}{5} =$

20) $10\frac{1}{2} \div 3\frac{1}{8} =$

21) $2\frac{1}{8} \div 1\frac{1}{2} =$

22) $1\frac{1}{10} \div 1\frac{3}{5} =$

23) $3\frac{2}{3} \div 2\frac{3}{4} =$

24) $2\frac{1}{2} \div 3\frac{2}{3} =$

25) $3\frac{3}{2} \div 1\frac{1}{7} =$

26) $3\frac{1}{24} \div 1\frac{1}{24} =$

Answers of Worksheets – Chapter 6

Fractions to Mixed Numbers

1) $3\frac{1}{3}$

2) $6\frac{1}{2}$

3) $7\frac{2}{3}$

4) $5\frac{1}{2}$

5) $4\frac{3}{5}$

6) $6\frac{1}{3}$

7) $5\frac{1}{4}$

8) $6\frac{2}{5}$

9) $1\frac{4}{9}$

10) $2\frac{4}{7}$

11) $6\frac{2}{7}$

12) $5\frac{2}{6}$

13) $3\frac{4}{5}$

14) $5\frac{3}{5}$

15) $7\frac{1}{2}$

16) $8\frac{1}{10}$

17) $12\frac{1}{2}$

18) $4\frac{4}{5}$

19) $4\frac{2}{3}$

20) $6\frac{4}{5}$

21) $5\frac{4}{5}$

22) $8\frac{7}{10}$

23) $5\frac{2}{3}$

24) $8\frac{1}{8}$

25) $6\frac{1}{2}$

26) $4\frac{3}{4}$

27) $7\frac{1}{5}$

28) $7\frac{1}{3}$

29) $5\frac{5}{8}$

30) $3\frac{2}{5}$

Mixed Numbers to Fractions

1) $\frac{9}{2}$

2) $\frac{8}{3}$

3) $\frac{5}{3}$

4) $\frac{11}{5}$

5) $\frac{42}{5}$

6) $\frac{7}{2}$

7) $\frac{23}{3}$

8) $\frac{7}{5}$

9) $\frac{37}{7}$

10) $\frac{14}{4}$

11) $\frac{26}{8}$

12) $\frac{16}{3}$

13) $\frac{26}{7}$

14) $\frac{11}{4}$

15) $\frac{61}{7}$

16) $\frac{50}{9}$

17) $\frac{89}{10}$

18) $\frac{41}{6}$

19) $\frac{51}{7}$

20) $\frac{39}{10}$

21) $\frac{17}{5}$

22) $\frac{19}{5}$

23) $\frac{23}{11}$

24) $\frac{9}{4}$

25) $\frac{20}{8}$

26) $\frac{44}{7}$

27) $\frac{19}{4}$

28) $\frac{76}{7}$

29) $\frac{97}{9}$

30) $\frac{6}{5}$

31) $\frac{56}{10}$

32) $\frac{243}{22}$

33) $\frac{75}{20}$

Add and Subtract Mixed Numbers with Like Denominators

1) $5\frac{1}{2}$

2) 7

3) $5\frac{4}{7}$

4) $4\frac{1}{3}$

5) $2\frac{17}{32}$

6) $6\frac{1}{16}$

7) $9\frac{7}{8}$

8) $7\frac{1}{36}$

9) $7\frac{1}{5}$

10) $13\frac{29}{60}$

11) 1

12) 1

13) $3\frac{1}{4}$ 17) $1\frac{2}{35}$ 21) $1\frac{3}{10}$ 25) $3\frac{19}{72}$

14) $\frac{5}{6}$ 18) $2\frac{23}{25}$ 22) $1\frac{3}{56}$ 26) $6\frac{1}{6}$

15) $6\frac{2}{5}$ 19) $7\frac{1}{24}$ 23) $1\frac{3}{4}$

16) $4\frac{1}{4}$ 20) $5\frac{1}{12}$ 24) $8\frac{4}{63}$

Adding and Subtracting Mixed Numbers

1) $20\frac{5}{16}$ 8) $8\frac{2}{3}$ 15) $1\frac{16}{39}$ 22) $\frac{11}{16}$

2) $8\frac{3}{4}$ 9) $9\frac{5}{8}$ 16) $1\frac{5}{26}$ 23) $1\frac{1}{3}$

3) $11\frac{11}{12}$ 10) $13\frac{13}{63}$ 17) $1\frac{5}{27}$ 24) $\frac{15}{22}$

4) $18\frac{1}{14}$ 11) $\frac{7}{16}$ 18) $\frac{62}{65}$ 25) $3\frac{15}{16}$

5) $11\frac{1}{121}$ 12) $1\frac{7}{10}$ 19) $1\frac{27}{128}$ 26) $2\frac{23}{25}$

6) $37\frac{5}{7}$ 13) $6\frac{3}{10}$ 20) $3\frac{9}{25}$

7) $9\frac{3}{4}$ 14) $1\frac{47}{258}$ 21) $1\frac{5}{12}$

Chapter 7:

Decimal

Topics that you'll practice in this chapter:

- ✓ Decimal Place Value

- ✓ Ordering and Comparing Decimals

- ✓ Decimal Addition

- ✓ Decimal Subtraction

Decimal Place Value

✍ What place is the selected digit?

1) 5,23<u>2</u>.25

2) 1,421.3<u>2</u>

3) 2,<u>2</u>59.91

4) 1,3<u>7</u>2.67

5) 1,215.<u>9</u>8

6) <u>5</u>,124.62

7) 1,365.8<u>9</u>

8) 3,770.<u>7</u>6

9) 7,<u>9</u>72.36

10) 1,24<u>9</u>.21

11) 2,21<u>6</u>.60

12) 3,1<u>9</u>1.88

13) <u>9</u>,263.31

14) 9,236.2<u>7</u>

15) 5,6<u>6</u>2.36

16) 2,26<u>8</u>.33

17) 7,787.<u>6</u>8

18) 2,<u>1</u>55.32

✍ What is the value of the selected digit?

19) 3,326.1<u>1</u>

20) 1,2<u>1</u>8.77

21) 5,562.<u>2</u>5

22) 4,<u>7</u>46.36

23) 8,8<u>3</u>3.36

24) 7,56<u>5</u>.36

25) 9,212.4<u>5</u>

26) <u>2</u>,535.82

27) 9,<u>4</u>51.36

28) 1,852.<u>2</u>4

Ordering and Comparing Decimals

✎ **Write the correct comparison symbol (>, < or =).**

1) 0.70 ☐ 0.070

2) 0.035 ☐ 0.35

3) 5.080 ☐ 5.09

4) 1.35 ☐ 1.02

5) 7.07 ☐ 0.770

6) 9.05 ☐ 9.5

7) 13.05 ☐ 13.050

8) 3.03 ☐ 3.1

9) 3.35 ☐ 3.225

10) 0.865 ☐ 0.0865

11) 5.18 ☐ 5.180

12) 0.818 ☐ 0.99

13) 10.080 ☐ 10.80

14) 6.68 ☐ 6.329

15) 5.33 ☐ 5.319

16) 2.15 ☐ 2.150

17) 1.76 ☐ 1.076

18) 10.051 ☐ 10.50

✎ **Order each set of integers from least to greatest.**

19) 0.5, 0.67, 0.25, 0.89, 0.39   ___, ___, ___, ___, ___, ___

20) 1.2, 3.8, 1.92, 5.87, 1.75   ___, ___, ___, ___, ___, ___

21) 3.3, 1.6, 1.8, 0.87, 0.55   ___, ___, ___, ___, ___, ___

22) 1.99, 1.8, 4.2, 6.2, 1.92, 4.55   ___, ___, ___, ___, ___, ___

Adding and Subtracting Decimals

✎ **Add and subtract decimals.**

1)
$$\begin{array}{r} 31.11 \\ -\ 21.45 \\ \hline \end{array}$$

4)
$$\begin{array}{r} 66.67 \\ -\ 34.39 \\ \hline \end{array}$$

7)
$$\begin{array}{r} 66.24 \\ -\ 23.11 \\ \hline \end{array}$$

2)
$$\begin{array}{r} 35.25 \\ +\ 14.47 \\ \hline \end{array}$$

5)
$$\begin{array}{r} 71.47 \\ +\ 16.25 \\ \hline \end{array}$$

8)
$$\begin{array}{r} 59.75 \\ +\ 22.85 \\ \hline \end{array}$$

3)
$$\begin{array}{r} 83.50 \\ +\ 12.78 \\ \hline \end{array}$$

6)
$$\begin{array}{r} 68.99 \\ -\ 33.61 \\ \hline \end{array}$$

9)
$$\begin{array}{r} 229.25 \\ -\ 84.67 \\ \hline \end{array}$$

✎ **Find the missing number.**

10) ___ $+ 5.2 = 7.5$

11) $2.8 +$ ___ $= 4.45$

12) $5.53 +$ ___ $= 9$

13) $5.23 -$ ___ $= 3.15$

14) ___ $- 4.75 = 7.32$

15) ___ $- 11.67 = 12.48$

16) $16.35 +$ ___ $= 19.78$

17) ___ $- 22.79 = 14.90$

18) ___ $+ 17.38 = 20.56$

19) $89.70 +$ ___ $= 106.50$

Multiplying and Dividing Decimals

✍ Find the product.

1) $0.8 \times 0.5 =$

2) $0.5 \times 0.4 =$

3) $2.25 \times 0.2 =$

4) $0.45 \times 0.4 =$

5) $1.48 \times 0.5 =$

6) $0.66 \times 0.3 =$

7) $4.62 \times 1.3 =$

8) $15.5 \times 7.2 =$

9) $20.6 \times 8.2 =$

10) $14.2 \times 4.5 =$

11) $26.1 \times 16.5 =$

12) $22.2 \times 2.2 =$

✍ Find the quotient.

13) $4.34 \div 100 =$

14) $88.1 \div 1,000 =$

15) $8.4 \div 2 =$

16) $9.2 \div 0.5 =$

17) $24.4 \div 0.2 =$

18) $35.5 \div 5 =$

19) $19.25 \div 100 =$

20) $48.8 \div 0.4 =$

21) $42.28 \div 0.1 =$

22) $36.12 \div 0.22 =$

23) $88.36 \div 0.8 =$

24) $76.78 \div 0.02 =$

Answers of Worksheets – Chapter 7

Decimal Place Value

1) ones

2) hundredths

3) hundreds

4) tens

5) tenths

6) thousands

7) hundredths

8) tenths

9) hundreds

10) ones

11) ones

12) tens

13) thousands

14) hundredths

15) tens

16) ones

17) tenths

18) hundreds

19) 0.01

20) 10

21) 0.2

22) 700

23) 30

24) 5

25) 0.05

26) 2,000

27) 400

28) 0.2

Order and Comparing Decimals

1) >

2) <

3) <

4) >

5) >

6) <

7) =

8) <

9) >

10) >

11) =

12) <

13) <

14) >

15) >

16) =

17) >

18) <

19) 0.25, 0.39, 0.5, 0.67, 0.89

20) 1.2, 1.75, 1.92, 3.8, 5.87

21) 0.55, 0.87, 1.6, 1.8, 3.3

22) 1.8, 1.92, 1.99, 4.2, 4.55, 6.2

Adding and Subtracting Decimals

1) 9.66	8) 82.60	15) 24.15
2) 49.72	9) 144.58	16) 3.43
3) 96.28	10) 2.3	17) 37.69
4) 32.28	11) 1.65	18) 3.18
5) 87.72	12) 3.47	19) 16.8
6) 35.38	13) 2.08	
7) 43.13	14) 12.07	

Multiplying and Dividing Decimals

1) 0.4	9) 168.92	17) 122
2) 0.2	10) 63.9	18) 7.1
3) 0.45	11) 430.65	19) 0.1925
4) 0.18	12) 48.84	20) 122
5) 0.74	13) 0.0434	21) 422.8
6) 0.198	14) 0.0881	22) 164.18
7) 6.006	15) 4.2	23) 110.45
8) 111.6	16) 18.4	24) 3,839

Chapter 8:
Proportions, Ratios, and Percent

Topics that you'll practice in this chapter:

- ✓ Simplifying Ratios

- ✓ Proportional Ratios

- ✓ Similarity and Ratios

- ✓ Ratio and Rates Word Problems

Simplifying Ratios

✎ Reduce each ratio.

1) $15 : 10 =$ ___ : ___

2) $6 : 60 =$ ___ : ___

3) $9 : 108 =$ ___ : ___

4) $12 : 24 =$ ___ : ___

5) $15 : 150 =$ ___ : ___

6) $10 : 30 =$ ___ : ___

7) $27 : 63 =$ ___ : ___

8) $16 : 32 =$ ___ : ___

9) $25 : 50 =$ ___ : ___

10) $28 : 36 =$ ___ : ___

11) $40 : 24 =$ ___ : ___

12) $81 : 27 =$ ___ : ___

13) $200 : 10 =$ ___ : ___

14) $16 : 40 =$ ___ : ___

15) $40 : 20 =$ ___ : ___

16) $70 : 35 =$ ___ : ___

17) $42 : 54 =$ ___ : ___

18) $72 : 18 =$ ___ : ___

19) $36 : 15 =$ ___ : ___

20) $18 : 3 =$ ___ : ___

21) $40 : 80 =$ ___ : ___

22) $28 : 49 =$ ___ : ___

23) $15 : 30 =$ ___ : ___

24) $7 : 70 =$ ___ : ___

✎ Write each ratio as a fraction in simplest form.

25) $5 : 10 =$

26) $18 : 60 =$

27) $10 : 70 =$

28) $20 : 110 =$

29) $16 : 48 =$

30) $18 : 84 =$

31) $8 : 32 =$

32) $60 : 400 =$

33) $45 : 108 =$

34) $54 : 246 =$

35) $44 : 72 =$

36) $18 : 36 =$

37) $7 : 56 =$

38) $22 : 121 =$

39) $36 : 540 =$

40) $72 : 216 =$

41) $48 : 84 =$

42) $36 : 240 =$

43) $110 : 205 =$

44) $24 : 960 =$

45) $30 : 150 =$

Proportional Ratios

✍ Fill in the blanks; solve each proportion.

1) $2:8 = \underline{\quad}:56$

2) $1:5 = 7:\underline{\quad}$

3) $1:12 = \underline{\quad}:24$

4) $8:7 = 16:\underline{\quad}$

5) $7:3 = 35:\underline{\quad}$

6) $6:2 = \underline{\quad}:18$

7) $20:1 = \underline{\quad}:20$

8) $1:7 = \underline{\quad}:49$

9) $10:1 = \underline{\quad}:20$

10) $5:4 = \underline{\quad}:32$

11) $3:12 = 12:\underline{\quad}$

12) $3:4 = 27:\underline{\quad}$

✍ State if each pair of ratios form a proportion.

13) $\frac{2}{10}$ and $\frac{5}{50}$

14) $\frac{1}{3}$ and $\frac{10}{30}$

15) $\frac{5}{3}$ and $\frac{35}{21}$

16) $\frac{2}{5}$ and $\frac{12}{40}$

17) $\frac{3}{4}$ and $\frac{27}{40}$

18) $\frac{3}{10}$ and $\frac{36}{72}$

19) $\frac{8}{10}$ and $\frac{56}{70}$

20) $\frac{1}{5}$ and $\frac{7}{35}$

21) $\frac{12}{17}$ and $\frac{48}{92}$

22) $\frac{10}{7}$ and $\frac{30}{35}$

23) $\frac{15}{10}$ and $\frac{45}{30}$

24) $\frac{25}{10}$ and $\frac{125}{50}$

✍ Solve each proportion.

25) $\frac{4}{10} = \frac{32}{x}$, $x = \underline{\quad}$

26) $\frac{1}{5} = \frac{7}{x}$, $x = \underline{\quad}$

27) $\frac{7}{5} = \frac{28}{x}$, $x = \underline{\quad}$

28) $\frac{1}{4} = \frac{x}{120}$, $x = \underline{\quad}$

29) $\frac{2}{5} = \frac{x}{45}$, $x = \underline{\quad}$

30) $\frac{1}{2} = \frac{16}{x}$, $x = \underline{\quad}$

31) $\frac{8}{7} = \frac{64}{x}$, $x = \underline{\quad}$

32) $\frac{11}{44} = \frac{32}{x}$, $x = \underline{\quad}$

33) $\frac{3}{7} = \frac{x}{77}$, $x = \underline{\quad}$

34) $\frac{3}{12} = \frac{x}{124}$, $x = \underline{\quad}$

35) $\frac{2}{13} = \frac{x}{78}$, $x = \underline{\quad}$

36) $\frac{7}{15} = \frac{x}{120}$, $x = \underline{\quad}$

Ratio and Rates Word Problems

✍ Solve each word problem.

1) Bob has 16 red cards and 40 green cards. What is the ratio of Bob's red cards to his green cards? _____

2) In a party, 20 soft drinks are required for every 24 guests. If there are 504 guests, how many soft drinks is required? _____

3) In Bob's class, 36 of the students are tall and 20 are short. In Mason's class 108 students are tall and 60 students are short. Which class has a higher ratio of tall to short students? _____

4) The price of 4 apples at the Quick Market is $1.92. The price of 10 of the same apples at Walmart is $5.00. Which place is the better buy? _____

5) The bakers at a Bakery can make 250 bagels in 5 hours. How many bagels can they bake in 12 hours? What is that rate per hour? _____

6) You can buy 15 cans of green beans at a supermarket for $9.20. How much does it cost to buy 45 cans of green beans? _____

7) The ratio of boys to girls in a class is 5:4. If there are 15 boys in the class, how many girls are in that class? _____

8) The ratio of red marbles to blue marbles in a bag is 2:5. If there are 49 marbles in the bag, how many of the marbles are red? _____

Answers of Worksheets – Chapter 8

Simplifying Ratios

1) 3 :2
2) 1 :10
3) 1 :12
4) 1 :2
5) 1 :10
6) 1 :3
7) 3 :7
8) 1 :2
9) 1 :2
10) 7 :9
11) 5 :3
12) 3 :1

13) 20 :1
14) 2 :5
15) 2 :1
16) 2 :1
17) 7 :9
18) 4 :1
19) 12 :5
20) 6 :1
21) 1 :2
22) 4 :7
23) 1 :2
24) 1 :10

25) 1/2
26) 3/10
27) 1/7
28) 2/11
29) 1/3
30) 3/14
31) 1/4
32) 3/20
33) 5/12
34) 9/41
35) 11/18
36) 1/2

37) 1/8
38) 2/11
39) 1/15
40) 1/3
41) 4/7
42) 3/20
43) 22/41
44) 1/4
45) 1/5

Proportional Ratios

1) 14
2) 35
3) 2
4) 14
5) 15
6) 54
7) 400
8) 7

9) 200
10) 40
11) 48
12) 36
13) No
14) Yes
15) Yes
16) No

17) No
18) No
19) Yes
20) Yes
21) No
22) No
23) Yes
24) Yes

25) 80
26) 35
27) 20
28) 30
29) 18
30) 32
31) 56
32) 128

33) 33	34) 31	35) 12	36) 56

Ratio and Rates Word Problems

1) 2:5

2) 420

3) The ratio for both classes is 9 to 5.

4) Quick Market is a better buy.

5) 600, the rate is 50per hour.

6) $27.60

7) 12

8) 14

Chapter 9: Measurement

Topics that you'll learn in this chapter:

✓ Reference Measurement

✓ Metric Length

✓ Customary Length

✓ Metric Capacity

✓ Customary Capacity

✓ Metric Weight and Mass

✓ Customary Weight and Mass

✓ Time

✓ Add Money Amounts

✓ Subtract Money Amounts

✓ Money: Word Problems

Reference Measurement

LENGTH	
Customary	**Metric**
1 mile (mi) = 1,760 yards (yd)	1 kilometer (km) = 1,000 meters (m)
1 yard (yd) = 3 feet (ft)	1 meter (m) = 100 centimeters (cm)
1 foot (ft) = 12 inches (in.)	1 centimeter(cm) = 10 millimeters(mm)
VOLUME AND CAPACITY	
Customary	**Metric**
1 gallon (gal) = 4 quarts (qt)	1 liter (L) = 1,000 milliliters (mL)
1 quart (qt) = 2 pints (pt.)	
1 pint (pt.) = 2 cups (c)	
1 cup (c) = 8 fluid ounces (Fl oz)	
WEIGHT AND MASS	
Customary	**Metric**
1 ton (T) = 2,000 pounds (lb.)	1 kilogram (kg) = 1,000 grams (g)
1 pound (lb.) = 16 ounces (oz)	1 gram (g) = 1,000 milligrams (mg)
Time	
1 year = 12 months	
1 year = 52 weeks	
1 week = 7 days	
1 day = 24 hours	
1 hour = 60 minutes	
1 minute = 60 seconds	

Metric Length Measurement

✍ Convert to the units.

1) 20 mm = _____ cm

2) 2 m = _____ mm

3) 7 m = _____ cm

4) 8 km = _____ m

5) 5,000 mm = _____ m

6) 600 cm = _____ m

7) 40 m = _____ cm

8) 3,000 mm = _____ cm

9) 9,000 mm = _____ m

10) 3 km = _____ mm

11) 40 km = _____ m

12) 70 m = _____ cm

13) 5,000 m = _____ km

14) 2,000 m = _____ km

Customary Length Measurement

✍ Convert to the units.

1) 9 ft = _____ in

2) 3 ft = _____ in

3) 7 yd = _____ ft

4) 16 yd = _____ ft

5) 4 yd = _____ in

6) 14 in = _____ ft

7) 432 in = ____ yd

8) 216 in = _____ yd

9) 57 yd = _____ in

10) 34 yd = _____ in

11) 72 ft = _____ yd

12) 240ft = _____ yd

13) 36 in = _____ ft

14) 59 yd = _____ feet

15) 15 in = _____ ft

16) 96 in = _____ ft

Metric Capacity Measurement

✍️**Convert the following measurements.**

1) 20 l = _____ ml

2) 9 l = _____ ml

3) 50 l = _____ ml

4) 44 l = _____ ml

5) 62 l = _____ ml

6) 17 l = _____ ml

7) 60,000 ml = _____ l

8) 25,000 ml = _____ l

9) 13,000 ml = _____ l

10) 7,000 ml = _____ l

11) 5,000 ml = _____ l

12) 35, 000 ml = _____ l

Customary Capacity Measurement

✍️**Convert the following measurements.**

1) 36 gal = _____ qt.

2) 42 gal = _____ pt.

3) 82 gal = _____ c.

4) 8 pt. = _____ c

5) 98 qt = _____ pt.

6) 17 qt = _____ c

7) 33 pt. = _____ c

8) 52 c = _____ gal

9) 288 pt. = _____ gal

10) 248 qt = _____ gal

11) 324 pt. = _____ qt

12) 100 c = _____ qt

13) 138 c = _____ pt.

14) 244 qt= _____ gal

15) 184 pt. = _____ qt

16) 36 gal = _____ pt.

17) 96qt = _____ c

18) 800 c = _____ gal

Metric Weight and Mass Measurement

✍ Convert.

1) 80 kg = _____ g

2) 77 kg = _____ g

3) 200 kg = _____ g

4) 60 kg = _____ g

5) 32 kg = _____ g

6) 90 kg = _____ g

7) 58 kg = _____ g

8) 26,000 g = _____ kg

9) 110,000 g = _____ kg

10) 400,000 g = _____ kg

11) 90,000 g = _____ kg

12) 10,000 g = _____ kg

13) 750,000 g = _____ kg

14) 500,000 g = _____ kg

Customary Weight and Mass Measurement

✍ Convert.

1) 16,000 lb. = _____ T

2) 40,000 lb. = _____ T

3) 8,000 lb. = _____ T

4) 32,000 lb. = _____ T

5) 60 lb. = _____ oz

6) 52 lb. = _____ oz

7) 70 lb. = _____ oz

8) 4 T = _____ lb.

9) 18 T = _____ lb.

10) 14 T = _____ lb.

11) 30 T = _____ lb.

12) 18 T = _____ oz

13) 7T = _____ oz

14) 6 T = _____ oz

15) 19 T = _____ lb

16) 24 T = _____ lb.

Temperature

✍Convert Fahrenheit into Celsius.

1) 5°F = ___ °C

2) 65°F= ___ °C

3) 122°F= ___ °C

4) 1.4°F= ___ °C

5) 95°F= ___ °C

6) 47.3°F= ___ °C

7) 140°F= ___ °C

8) 55.4°F= ___ °C

9) 120°F= ___ °C

10) 132°F= ___ °C

11) 158°F= ___ °C

12) 114.8°F= ___ °C

✍Convert Celsius into Fahrenheit.

13) 35°C = ___ °F

14) 20°C = ___ °F

15) 60°C = ___°F

16) 50°C = ___ °F

17) 17°C = ___ °F

18) 45°C = ___ °F

19) 10°C = ___ °F

20) 23°C = ___°F

21) 29°C = ___ °F

22) 60°C = ___ °F

23) 56°C = ___°F

24) 2°C = ___°F

Time

✎Convert to the units.

1) 20 hr = _____ min

2) 12 year = _____ week

3) 5 hr = _____ sec

4) 75 min = _____ sec

5) 1200 min = _____ hr

6) 730 day = _____ year

7) 2 year = _____ hr

8) 40 day = _____ hr

9) 2 day = _____ min

10) 480 min = _____ hr

11) 30 year = _____ month

12) 3600 sec = _____ min

13) 168 hr = _____ day

14) 18 weeks = _____ day

✎How much time has passed?

1) From 3:15 A.M. to 6:25 A.M.: ____ hours and ___ minutes.

2) From 2:20 A.M. to 7:05 A.M.: ____ hours and ___ minutes.

3) It's 8:30 P.M. What time was 4 hours ago? _____ O'clock

4) 3:10 A.M to 6:30 AM: _____ hours and _____ minutes.

5) 4:35 A.M to 7:10 AM: _____ hours and _____ minutes.

6) 8:00 A.M. to 9:25 AM. = _____ hour(s) and _____ minutes.

7) 11:45 A.M. to 4:15 PM. = _____ hour(s) and _____ minutes

8) 7:15 A.M. to 7:50 A.M. = _____ minutes

9) 4:05 A.M. to 4:52 A.M. = _____ minutes

Money Amounts

✍ Add.

1)
$314
+$132
_____

$524
+$410
_____

$390
+$215
_____

2)
$521
+$330
_____

$630
+$321
_____

$732
+$145
_____

3)
$511
+$212
_____

$660
+$128
_____

$830
+$110
_____

4)
$721.60
+$63.70
_____

$221.20
+$220.75
_____

$515.00
+$456.30
_____

✍ Subtract.

5)
$836
−$155
_____

$642
−$111
_____

$733
−$533
_____

6)
$438
−$136
_____

$498
−$326
_____

$740
−$549
_____

7)
$356.40
−$219.70
_____

$710.50
−$128.80
_____

$832.70
−$379.20
_____

8) Linda had $14.00. She bought some game tickets for $7.14.
How much did she have left?

Money: Word Problems

✎**Solve.**

1) How many boxes of envelopes can you buy with $48 if one box costs $6?

2) After paying $8.15 for a salad, Ella has $44.36. How much money did she have before buying the salad?

3) How many packages of diapers can you buy with $90 if one package costs $6?

4) Last week James ran 30 miles more than Michael. James ran 56 miles. How many miles did Michael run?

5) Last Friday Jacob had $32.52. Over the weekend he received some money for cleaning the attic. He now has $51. How much money did he receive?

6) After paying $12.12 for a sandwich, Amelia has $47.50. How much money did she have before buying the sandwich?

Answers of Worksheets – Chapter 9

Metric length

1) 2 cm

2) 2,000 mm

3) 700 cm

4) 8,000 m

5) 5 m

6) 6 m

7) 4,000 cm

8) 30 cm

9) 9 m

10) 3,000,000 mm

11) 40,000 m

12) 7,000 cm

13) 5 km

14) 2 km

Customary Length

1) 108

2) 36

3) 21

4) 48

5) 144

6) 1.17

7) 12

8) 6

9) 2,052

10) 1,224

11) 24

12) 80

13) 3

14) 177

15) 1.25

16) 8

Metric Capacity

1) 20,000 ml

2) 9,000 ml

3) 50,000 ml

4) 44,000 ml

5) 62,000 ml

6) 17,000 ml

7) 60 L

8) 25 L

9) 13 L

10) 7 L

11) 5 L

12) 35 L

Customary Capacity

1) 144 qt

2) 336 pt.

3) 1312 c

4) 16 c

5) 196 pt.

6) 68 c

7) 66 c

8) 3.25 gal

9) 36 gal

10) 62 gal

11) 162 qt

12) 25qt

13) 69 pt.

14) 61 gal

15) 92 qt

16) 288 pt.

17) 384 c

18) 50gal

Metric Weight and Mass

1) 80,000 g

2) 77,000 g

3) 200,000 g

4) 60,000 g

5) 32,000 g

6) 90,000 g

7) 58,000 g

8) 26 kg

9) 110 kg

10) 400 kg

11) 90 kg

12) 10 kg

13) 750 kg
14) 500 kg

Customary Weight and Mass

1) 8 T
2) 20 T
3) 4 T
4) 16 T
5) 960 oz
6) 832 oz

7) 1,120 oz
8) 8,000 lb.
9) 36,000 lb.
10) 28,000 lb.
11) 60,000 lb.
12) 576,000 oz

13) 224,000 oz
14) 192,000 oz
15) 38,000 lb
16) 48,000 lb

Temperature

1) −15°C
2) 18.3°C
3) 50°C
4) −17°C
5) 35°C
6) 8.5°C
7) 60°C
8) 13°C

9) 48.9°C
10) 55.6°C
11) 70°C
12) 46°C
13) 95°F
14) 68°F
15) 140°F
16) 122°F

17) 62.6°F
18) 113°F
19) 50°F
20) 73.4°F
21) 84.2°F
22) 140°F
23) 132.8°F
24) 35.6°F

Time - Convert

1) 1,200 min
2) 624 weeks
3) 18,000 sec
4) 4,500 sec
5) 20 hr

6) 2 year
7) 17,520 hr
8) 960 hr
9) 2,880 min
10) 8 hr

11) 360 months
12) 60 min
13) 7 days
14) 126 days

Time - Gap

1) 3:10
2) 4:45
3) 4:30 P.M.

4) 3:20
5) 2:35
6) 1:25

7) 4:30
8) 35 minutes
9) 47 minutes

Add Money

1) 446, 934, 605
2) 851, 951, 877

3) 723, 788, 940
4) 785.30, 441.95, 971.30

Subtract Money

5) 681–531–200

6) 302–172–191

7) 136.70–581.70–453.50

8) $6.86

Money: word problem

1) 8

2) $52.51

3) 15

4) 26

5) 18.48

6) 59.62

Chapter 10:
Symmetry and Three-Dimensional Figures

Topics that you'll practice in this chapter:

✓ Line Segments

✓ Identify Lines of Symmetry

✓ Count Lines of Symmetry

✓ Parallel, Perpendicular and Intersecting Lines

✓ Identify Three–Dimensional Figures

✓ Count Vertices, Edges, and Faces

✓ Identify Faces of Three–Dimensional Figures

Line Segments

✎ **Write each as a line, ray or line segment.**

1)

2)

3)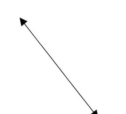

4)

5)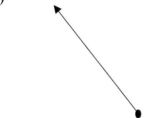

6)

7)

8)

Parallel, Perpendicular and Intersecting Lines

✐ State whether the given pair of lines are parallel, perpendicular, or intersecting.

1)

2)

3)
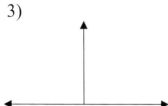

4)
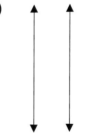

5)
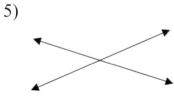

6)
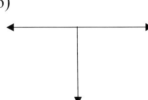

7)
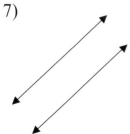

8)
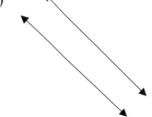

Identify Lines of Symmetry

✍ **Tell whether the line on each shape a line of symmetry is.**

1)

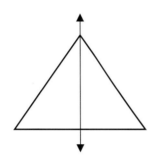

2)

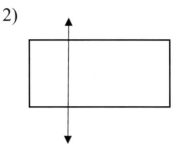

3)

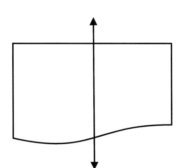

4)

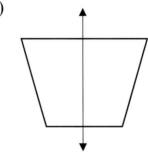

5)

6)

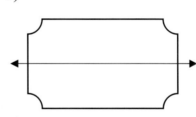

7)

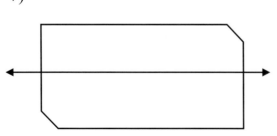

8)

Lines of Symmetry

✍ **Draw lines of symmetry on each shape. Count and write the lines of symmetry you see.**

1)

2)

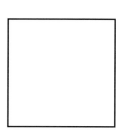

3)

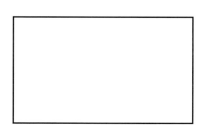

4)

5)

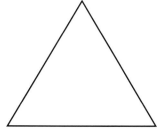

6)

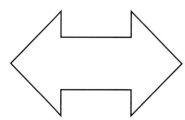

7)

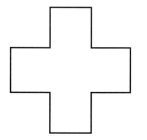

8)

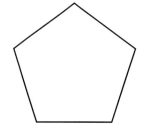

Identify Three–Dimensional Figures

✍ **Write the name of each shape.**

1)

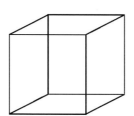

2)

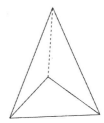

3)

4)

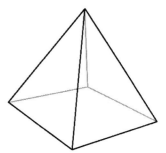

5)

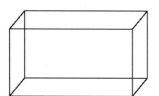

6)

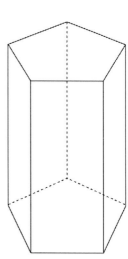

7)

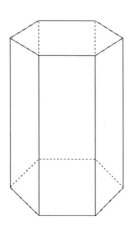

Vertices, Edges, and Faces

✎ Complete the chart below.

Shape	Number of edges	Number of faces	Number of vertices
1)	_____	_____	_____
2)	_____	_____	_____
3)	_____	_____	_____
4)	_____	_____	_____
5)	_____	_____	_____
6)	_____	_____	_____

Identify Faces of Three–Dimensional Figures

✎ **Write the number of faces.**

1)

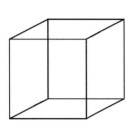

2)

3)

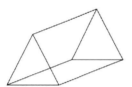

4)

5)

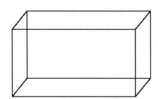

6)

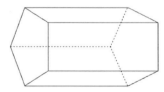

7)

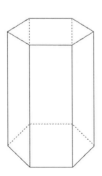

8)

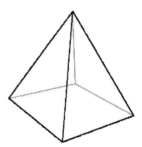

Answers of Worksheets – Chapter 10

Line Segments

1) Line segment

2) Ray

3) Line

4) Line segment

5) Ray

6) Line

7) Line

8) Line segment

Parallel, Perpendicular and Intersecting Lines

1) Parallel

2) Intersection

3) Perpendicular

4) Parallel

5) Intersection

6) Perpendicular

7) Parallel

8) Parallel

Identify lines of symmetry

1) yes

2) no

3) no

4) yes

5) yes

6) yes

7) no

8) yes

lines of symmetry

1)

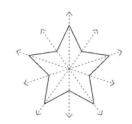

2)

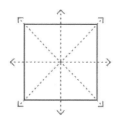

3)

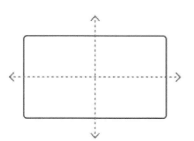

4)

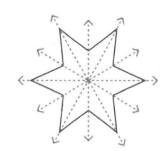

5)

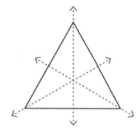

6)

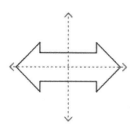

7)

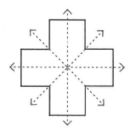

8)

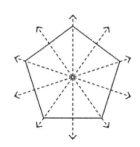

Identify Three–Dimensional Figures

1) Cube

2) Triangular pyramid

3) Triangular prism

4) Square pyramid

5) Rectangular prism

6) Pentagonal prism

7) Hexagonal prism

Vertices, Edges, and Faces

	Shape	Number of edges	Number of faces	Number of vertices
1)		6	4	4
8)		8	5	5
9)		12	6	8

10)    12   6   8

11)    15   7   10

12) 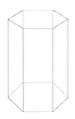   18   8   12

Identify Faces of Three–Dimensional Figures

1) 6   4) 4   7) 8

2) 2   5) 6   8) 5

3) 5   6) 7

Chapter 11:

Geometric

Topics that you'll practice in this chapter:

- ✓ Identifying Angles: Acute, Right, Obtuse, and Straight Angles

- ✓ Polygon Names

- ✓ Triangles

- ✓ Quadrilaterals and Rectangles

- ✓ Perimeter: Find the Missing Side Lengths

- ✓ Perimeter and Area of Squares

- ✓ Perimeter and Area of rectangles

- ✓ Area and Perimeter: Word Problems

- ✓ Area of Squares and Rectangles

- ✓ Volume of Cubes and Rectangle Prisms

Identifying Angles

✎ **Write the name of the angles(Acute, Right, Obtuse, and Straight Angles).**

1)

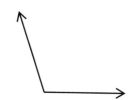

2)

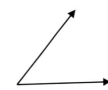

3)

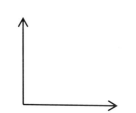

4)

5)

6)

7)

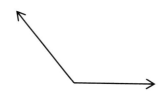

8)

Polygon Names

 **Write name of polygons.**

1)

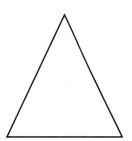

2)

3)

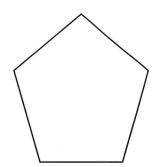

4)

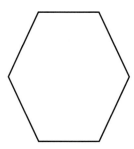

5)

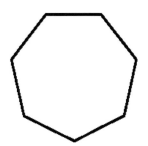

6)

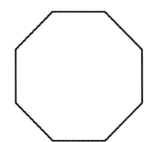

7)

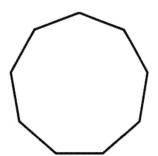

8)

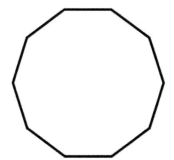

Triangles

✎ Classify the triangles by their sides and angles.

1)

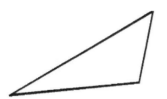

2)

3)

4)

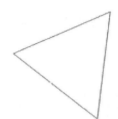

5)

6)

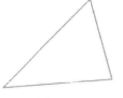

✎Find the measure of the unknown angle in each triangle.

7)

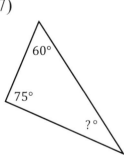

8)

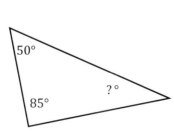

9)

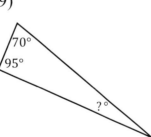

10)

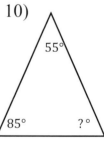

11)

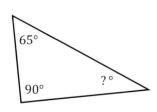

12)

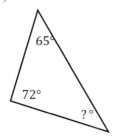

13)

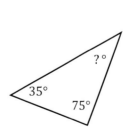

14)

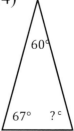

Quadrilaterals and Rectangles

✎ **Write the name of quadrilaterals.**

1)   2)   3)

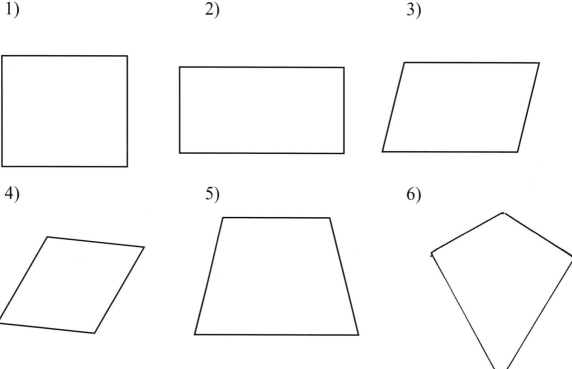

4)   5)   6)

✎ **Solve.**

7) A rectangle has _____ sides and _____ angles.

8) Draw a rectangle that is 6 centimeters long and 5 centimeters wide. What is the perimeter?

9) Draw a rectangle 5 cm long and 3 cm wide.

10) Draw a rectangle whose length is 6cm and whose width is 4 cm. What is the perimeter of the rectangle?

11) What is the perimeter of the rectangle?

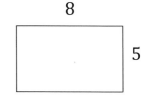

8

5

Perimeter: Find the Missing Side Lengths

✎ **Find the missing side of each shape.**

1) perimeter = 44

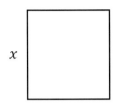

2) perimeter = 36

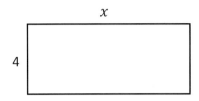

3) perimeter = 24

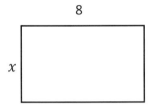

4) perimeter = 28

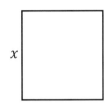

5) perimeter = 160

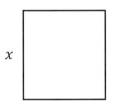

6) perimeter = 44

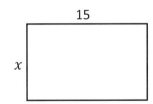

7) perimeter = 42

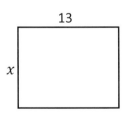

8) perimeter = 36

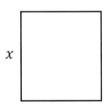

9) perimeter = 90

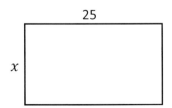

10)   perimeter = 20

Perimeter and Area of Squares

 **Find perimeter and area of squares.**

1) A: _____, P: _____

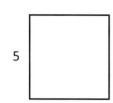
5

2) A: _____, P: _____

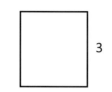
3

3) A: _____, P: _____

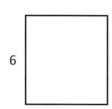
6

4) A: _____, P: _____

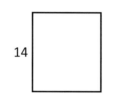
14

5) A: _____, P: _____

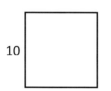
10

6) A: _____, P: _____

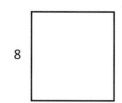
8

7) A: _____, P: _____

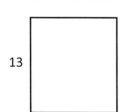
13

8) A: _____, P: _____

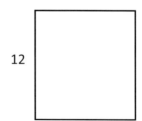
12

9) A: _____, P: _____

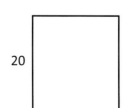
20

10) A: _____, P: _____

4

Perimeter and Area of rectangles

 **Find perimeter and area of rectangles.**

1) A: ___, P: ___

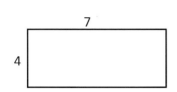

2) A: ___, P: ___

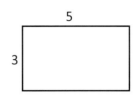

3) A: ___, P: ___

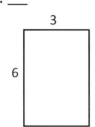

4) A: ___, P: ___

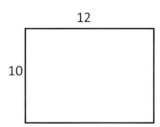

5) A: ___, P: ___

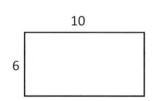

6) A: ___, P: ___

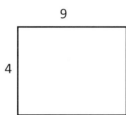

7) A: ___, P: ___

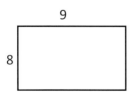

8) A: ___, P: ___

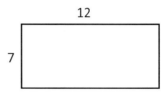

9) A: ___, P: ___

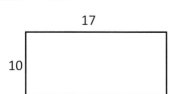

10) A: ___, P: ___

Find the Area or Missing Side Length of a Rectangle

✎ **Find area or missing side length of rectangles.**

1) Area =?

10

4

2) Area = 56, x =?

x

7

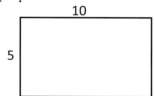

3) Area = $80_8 x$ =?

x

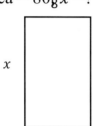

4) Area =?

10

5

5) Area =?

23

13

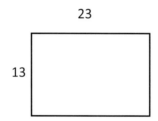

6) Area = 1200, x =?

20

x

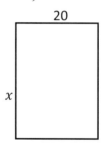

7) Area = 540, x =?

36

x

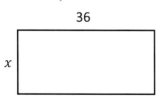

8) Area = 391, x =?

x

17

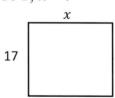

9) Area = 180, x =?

15

x

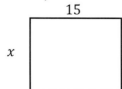

10) Area = 1,125, x =?

x

25

Area and Perimeter

✎ **Find the area of each.**

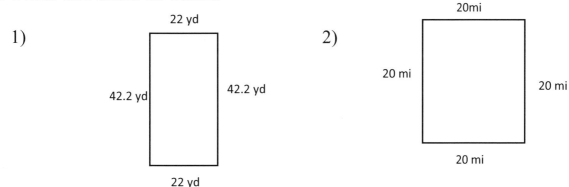

1) 22 yd / 42.2 yd / 42.2 yd / 22 yd

2) 20mi / 20 mi / 20 mi / 20 mi

✎ **Solve.**

3) The area of a rectangle is 72 square meters. The width is 8 meters. What is the length of the rectangle?

4) A square has an area of 64 square feet. What is the perimeter of the square?

5) Ava built a rectangular vegetable garden that is 7 feet long and has an area of 42 square feet. What is the perimeter of Ava's vegetable garden?

6) A square has a perimeter of 52 millimeters. What is the area of the square?

7) The perimeter of David's square backyard is 84 meters. What is the area of David's backyard?

8) The area of a rectangle is 45 square inches. The length is 5 inches. What is the perimeter of the rectangle?

Volume of Cubes

✏️ Find the volume of each cube.

1)

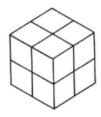

2)

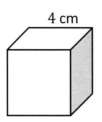

3)

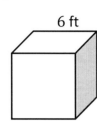

4)

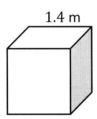

5)

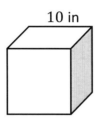

6)

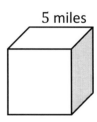

7)

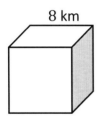

8)

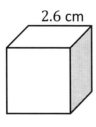

9)

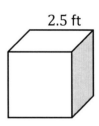

10)

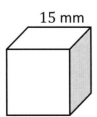

11)

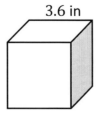

12)

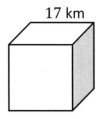

Answers of Worksheets – Chapter 11

Identifying Angles

1) Obtuse
2) Acute
3) Right
4) Acute
5) Straight
6) Obtuse
7) Obtuse
8) Acute

Polygon Names

1) Triangle
2) Quadrilateral
3) Pentagon
4) Hexagon
5) Heptagon
6) Octagon
7) Nonagon
8) Decagon

Triangles

1) Scalene, obtuse
2) Isosceles, right
3) Scalene, right
4) Equilateral, acute
5) Scalene, acute
6) Scalene, acute
7) $45°$
8) $45°$
9) $15°$
10) $40°$
11) $25°$
12) $43°$
13) $70°$
14) $53°$

Quadrilaterals and Rectangles

1) Square
2) Rectangle
3) Parallelogram
4) Rhombus
5) Trapezoid
6) Kike
7) 4 - 4
8) 22
9) Use a rule to draw the rectangle
10) 20
11) 26

Perimeter: Find the Missing Side Lengths

1) 11
2) 14
3) 4
4) 7
5) 40
6) 7
7) 8
8) 9
9) 20
10) 8

Perimeter and Area of Squares

1) A:25, P: 20
2) A: 9, P: 12
3) A: 36, P: 24
4) A: 196, P: 56
5) A: 100, P: 40
6) A: 64, P: 32
7) A: 169, P: 52
8) A: 144, P: 48
9) A: 400, P: 80
10) A: 16, P: 16

Perimeter and Area of rectangles

1) A: 28, P: 22
2) A: 15, P: 16
3) A: 18, P: 18
4) A: 120, P: 44
5) A: 60, P: 32
6) A: 36, P: 26
7) A: 72, P: 34
8) A: 84, P: 38
9) A: 170, P: 54
10) A: 65, P: 36

Find the Area or Missing Side Length of a Rectangle

1) 40
2) 8
3) 10
4) 50
5) 299
6) 60
7) 15
8) 23
9) 12
10) 45

Area and Perimeter

1) $928.4 \, yd^2$
2) $400 \, mi^2$
3) 9
4) 32
5) 26
6) 169
7) 441
8) 28

Volume of Cubes

1) 8
2) $64 \, cm^3$
3) $216 \, ft^3$
4) $2.744 \, m^3$
5) $1,000 \, in^2$
6) $125 \, miles^3$
7) $512 \, km^3$
8) $17.576 \, cm^3$
9) $15.625 \, ft^3$
10) $3,375 \, mm^3$
11) $46.656 \, in^3$
12) $4,913 km^3$

Chapter 12:

Data and Graphs

Topics that you'll practice in this chapter:

- ✓ Graph Points on a Coordinate Plane

- ✓ Bar Graph

- ✓ Tally and Pictographs

- ✓ Line Graphs

- ✓ Stem–And–Leaf Plot

- ✓ Scatter Plots

Graph Points on a Coordinate Plane

✎ **Plot each point on the coordinate grid.**

1) A $(2,7)$

2) B $(6,3)$

3) C $(0,7)$

4) D $(3,0)$

5) E $(1,4)$

6) F $(3,9)$

7) G $(5,1)$

8) H $(7,7)$

9) I $(9,6)$

10) J $(6,1)$

11) K $(2,4)$

12) L $(3,8)$

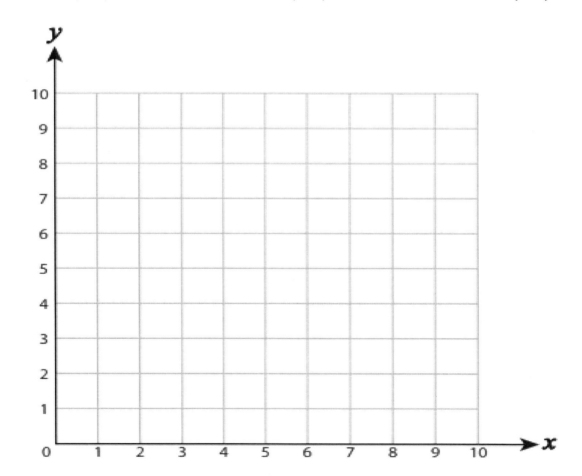

Bar Graph

✎ **Graph the given information as a bar graph.**

Day	Hot dogs sold
Monday	70
Tuesday	30
Wednesday	50
Thursday	10
Friday	60

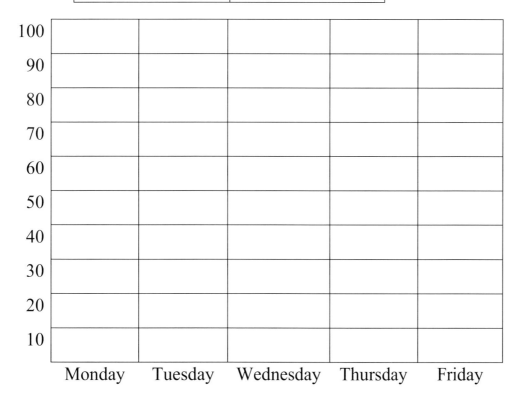

Tally and Pictographs

✎ **Using the key, draw the pictograph to show the information.**

Key: 😊 = 2 animals

Line Graphs

✍ David work as a salesman in a store. He records the number of phones sold in five days on a line graph. Use the graph to answer the questions.

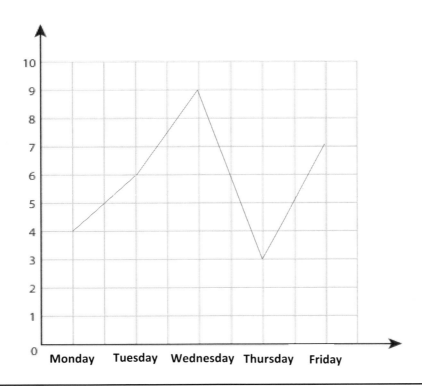

1) How many phones were sold on Tuesday?

2) Which day had the minimum sales of phones?

3) Which day had the maximum number of phones sold?

4) How many phones were sold in 5 days?

Time Series

✍ **Use the following Graph to complete the table.**

Day	Distance (km)
1	
2	

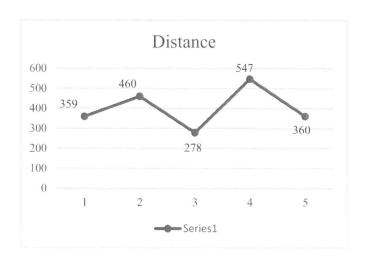

The following table shows the number of births in the US from 2007 to 2012 (in millions).

Year	Number of births (in millions)
2007	4.32
2008	4.25
2009	4.13
2010	4
2011	3.95
2012	3.95

Draw a time series for the table.

Answers of Worksheets – Chapter 12

Graph Points on a Coordinate Plane

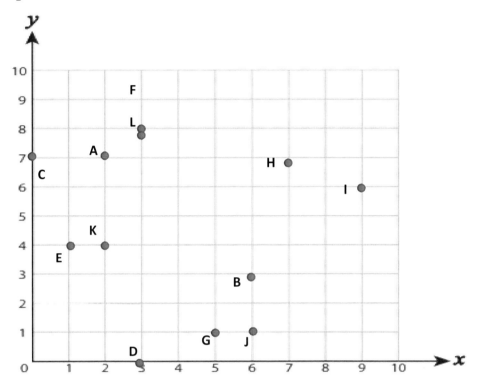

Bar Graph

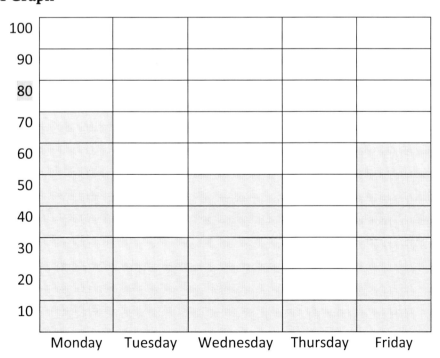

Tally and Pictographs

Line Graphs

1) 6   2) Thursday   3) Wednesday   4) 29

Time Series

Day	Distance (km)
1	359
2	460
3	278
4	547
5	360

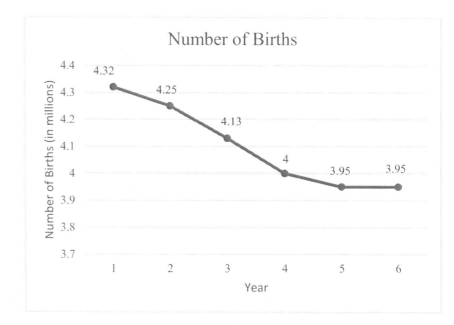

PSSA Math Practice Tests

Time to Test

Time to refine your skill with a practice examination

Take a REAL PSSA Mathematics test to simulate the test day experience. After you've finished, score your test using the answer key.

Before You Start

- You'll need a pencil and scratch papers to take the test.
- For this practice test, don't time yourself. Spend time as much as you need.
- It's okay to guess. You won't lose any points if you're wrong.
- After you've finished the test, review the answer key to see where you went wrong.

Calculators are not permitted for Grade 5 PSSA Tests

Good Luck!

Grade 5 PSSA Mathematics Formula Sheet

Formulas that you may need to work questions on this test are found below. You may refer to this page at any time during the mathematics test.

Standard Conversions

1 mile (mi) = 1,760 yards (yd)
1 mile = 5,280 feet (ft)
1 yard (yd) = 3 feet (ft)
1 foot = 12 inches (in.)

1 ton (T) = 2,000 pounds (lb)
1 pound = 16 ounces (oz.)

1 gallon (gal) = 4 quarts (qt)
1 quart = 2 pints (pt)
1 pint = 2 cups (c)
1 cup = 8 fluid ounces (fl oz.)

Metric Conversions

1 kilometer (km) = 1,000 meters (m)
1 meter = 100 centimeters (cm)
1 centimeter = 10 millimeters (mm)

1 kilogram (kg) = 1,000 grams (g)

1 liter (L) = 1,000 milliliters (mL)

Time Conversions

1 century = 10 decades
1 decade = 10 years (yr)
1 year (yr) = 12 months (mo)
1 year = 52 weeks (wk)
1 year = 365 days
1 week = 7 days
1 day = 24 hours (hr)
1 hour = 60 minutes (min)
1 minute = 60 seconds (sec)

Rectangular Prism

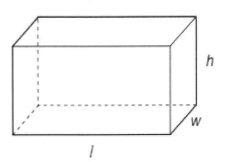

Volume = length × width × height
$V = l \times w \times h$

Volume = area of the base × height
$V = B \times h$

Volume = area of the base × width
$V = B \times w$

Volume = area of the base × length
$V = B \times l$

The Pennsylvania System of School Assessment PSSA Practice Test 1

Mathematics

GRADE 5

- ❖ 20 Questions
- ❖ Calculators are permitted for this practice test

Pennsylvania Department of Education Bureau of Curriculum, Assessment

and Instruction— *Month Year*

1) A baker uses 5 eggs to bake a cake. How many cakes will he be able to bake with 260 eggs?

    A. 60

    B. 52

    C. 54

    D. 42

2) The area of a rectangle is D square feet and its length is 11 feet. Which equation represents W, the width of the rectangle in feet?

    A. $W = \dfrac{D}{11}$

    B. $W = \dfrac{11}{D}$

    C. $W = 11D$

    D. $W = 11 + D$

3) Which list shows the fractions in order from least to greatest?

$$\frac{3}{5}, \frac{8}{9}, \frac{3}{10}, \frac{3}{4}, \frac{5}{11}$$

    A. $\dfrac{3}{4}, \dfrac{8}{9}, \dfrac{3}{10}, \dfrac{3}{5}, \dfrac{5}{11}$

    B. $\dfrac{5}{11}, \dfrac{3}{5}, \dfrac{3}{4}, \dfrac{8}{9}, \dfrac{3}{10}$

    C. $\dfrac{3}{10}, \dfrac{3}{4}, \dfrac{8}{9}, \dfrac{3}{5}, \dfrac{5}{11}$

    D. $\dfrac{3}{10}, \dfrac{5}{11}, \dfrac{3}{5}, \dfrac{3}{4}, \dfrac{8}{9}$

4) If A = 35, then which of the following equations are correct?

    A. A + 35 = 70

    B. A ÷ 35 = 70

    C. 35 × A = 70

    D. A − 35 = 70

5) Which statement about 7 multiplied by $\frac{3}{2}$ is true?

    A. The product is between 5 and 7

    B. The product is between 9 and 11

    C. The product is more than $\frac{23}{2}$

    D. The product is between $\frac{12}{5}$ and 8

6) The area of a circle is 64π. What is the circumference of the circle?

    A. 8 π

    B. 16 π

    C. 25 π

    D. 64 π

7) What is the volume of this box?

    A. 63 cm^3

    B. 112 cm^3

    C. 278 cm^3

    D. 378 cm^3

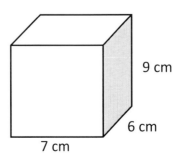

9 cm

6 cm

7 cm

8) A shirt costing $140 is discounted 15%. Which of the following expressions can be used to find the selling price of the shirt?

A. (140) (0.15)

B. (140) – 140 (0.85)

C. (140) (0.15) – (140) (0.15)

D. (140) (0.85)

9) In a bag, there are 60 cards. Of these cards, 12 cards are white. What fraction of the cards are white?

A. $\frac{1}{5}$

B. $\frac{3}{10}$

C. $\frac{5}{60}$

D. $\frac{5}{10}$

10) The perimeter of the trapezoid below is 58. What is its area?

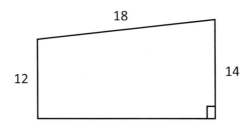

Write your answer in the box below.

11) A rope weighs 400 grams per meter of length. What is the weight in kilograms of 14.5 meters of this rope? (1 kilograms = 1000 grams)

A. 0.058

B. 0.58

C. 5.8

D. 5,800

12) 13 yards 5 feet and 6 inches equals to how many inches?

A. 60

B. 434

C. 534

D. 468

13) Which expression has a value of – 5?

A. $2 + (– 15) – (– 8)$

B. $4 + (– 2) \times (– 5)$

C. $– 5 \times (– 3) + (– 4) \times (– 10)$

D. $3 \times (– 5) + 8$

14) Of the 2,500 videos available for rent at a certain video store, 750 are comedies. What percent of the videos are comedies?

A. 1.30%

B. 0.30%

C. 30%

D. 130%

15) The length of a rectangle is $\frac{3}{8}$ of inches and the width of the rectangle is $\frac{4}{15}$ of inches. What is the area of that rectangle?

A. $\frac{3}{10}$

B. $\frac{1}{10}$

C. $\frac{10}{15}$

D. $\frac{1}{5}$

16) William keeps track of the length of each fish that he catches. Following are the lengths in inches of the fish that he caught one day: 32, 16,19, 24, 16, 21,7

What is the median fish length that William caught that day?

A. 32 Inches

B. 24 Inches

C. 16 Inches

D. 19 Inches

17) Solve. $\frac{1}{3} + \frac{7}{9} - \frac{5}{18} =$

A. $\frac{9}{14}$

B. $\frac{5}{8}$

C. $\frac{5}{6}$

D. 1

18) If one acre of forest contains 170 pine trees, how many pine trees are contained in 20 acres?

    A. 3,400

    B. 340

    C. 4,300

    D. 34,000

19) How many $\frac{1}{3}$ cup servings are in a package of cheese that contains $4\frac{1}{3}$ cups altogether?

    A. $4\frac{1}{2}$

    B. $\frac{13}{3}$

    C. 26

    D. 13

20) The area of the base of the following cylinder is 40 square inches and its height is 9 inches. What is the volume of the cylinder?

    Write your answer in the box below.

"This is the end of Practice Test 1"

The Pennsylvania System of School Assessment
PSSA Practice Test 2

Mathematics

GRADE 5

❖ 20 Questions

❖ Calculators are permitted for this practice test

Pennsylvania Department of Education Bureau of Curriculum, Assessment

and Instruction— *Month Year*

1) Jack added 15 to the product of 17 and 21. What is this sum?

    A. 57

    B. 324

    C. 372

    D. 3,452

2) Joe makes $3.95 per hour at his work. If he works 9 hours, how much money will he earn?

    A. $35.00

    B. $35.75

    C. $39.50

    D. $35.55

3) Which of the following is an obtuse angle?

    A. 69°

    B. 60°

    C. 130°

    D. 250°

4) What is the value of $8 - 4\frac{3}{5}$?

    A. $\frac{23}{5}$

    B. $3\frac{2}{5}$

    C. $-\frac{1}{5}$

    D. $\frac{40}{17}$

5) The bride and groom invited 250 guests for their wedding. 203 guests arrived. What percent of the guest list was not present?

A. 48%

B. 18.87%

C. 47.52%

D. 18.8%

6) In a party, 9 soft drinks are required for every 18 guests. If there are 216 guests, how many soft drinks are required?

A. 98

B. 38

C. 108

D. 178

7) You are asked to chart the temperature during an 8–hour period to give the average. These are your results:

7 am: 6 degrees   11 am: 35 degrees

8 am: 9 degrees   12 pm: 37 degrees

9 am: 21 degrees   1 pm: 37 degrees

10 am: 24 degrees   2 pm: 39 degrees

What is the average temperature?

A. 26

B. 24

C. 37

D. 47

8) While at work, Emma checks her email once every 120 minutes. In 16 hours, how many times does she check her email?

A. 10 Times

B. 8 Times

C. 5 Times

D. 6 Times

9) A florist has 492 flowers. How many full bouquets of 12 flowers can he make?

A. 43

B. 46

C. 42

D. 41

10) What is 5,198.48525 rounded to the nearest tenth?

A. 5,198.485

B. 5,198.5

C. 5,198

D. 5,198.48

11) If a rectangular swimming pool has a perimeter of 108 feet and it is 28 feet wide, what is its area?

A.1,456 square feet

B.2,840 square feet

C.1,232 square feet

D.728 square feet

12) What is the volume of the following rectangle prism?

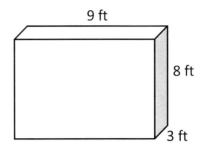

    A. $24\ ft^3$

    B. $206\ ft^3$

    C. $72\ ft^3$

    D. $216 ft^3$

13) A circle has a diameter of 8 inches. What is its approximate circumference? (π = 3.14)

    A. 12.46 inches

    B. 25.12 inches

    C. 65.30 inches

    D. 50.24 inches

14) How long is the line segment shown on the number line below?

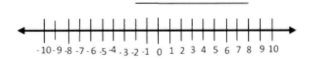

    A. 10

    B. 8

    C. 6

    D. 12

15) Peter traveled 140 miles in 7 hours and Jason traveled 300 miles in 6 hours. What is the ratio of the average speed of Peter to average speed of Jason?

A. 2: 5

B. 7: 16

C. 7: 6

D. 2: 7

16) If $x = -3$, which equation is true?

A. $x(3x - 5) = 45$

B. $5(3 - x) = 30$

C. $4(2x + 1) = 16$

D. $7x - 4 = -28$

17) What are the coordinates of the intersection of $x-axis$ and the $y-axis$ on a coordinate plane?

A. $(0, -1)$

B. $(1, 0)$

C. $(0, 0)$

D. $(0, 1)$

18) In a triangle ABC the measure of angle ACB is $45°$ and the measure of angle CAB is $95°$. What is the measure of angle ABC?

Write your answer in the box below.

19) Which list shows the fractions listed in order from least to greatest?

$$\frac{1}{4}, \frac{1}{11}, \frac{1}{9}, \frac{1}{5}$$

A. $\frac{1}{9}, \frac{1}{4}, \frac{1}{11}, \frac{1}{5}$

B. $\frac{1}{5}, \frac{1}{11}, \frac{1}{4}, \frac{1}{9}$

C. $\frac{1}{4}, \frac{1}{5}, \frac{1}{9}, \frac{1}{11}$

D. $\frac{1}{11}, \frac{1}{9}, \frac{1}{5}, \frac{1}{4}$

20) Aria was hired to teach four identical 5th grade math courses, which entailed being present in the classroom 28 hours altogether. At $25 per class hour, how much did Aria earn for teaching one course?

A. $75

B. $175

C. $250

D. $1,125

"This is the end of Practice Test 2"

Answers and Explanations

PSSA Practice Tests

Answer Key

❋ Now, it's time to review your results to see where you went wrong and what areas you need to improve!

PSSA - Mathematics

Practice Test - 1				Practice Test - 2			
1	B	11	C	1	C	11	D
2	A	12	C	2	D	12	D
3	D	13	A	3	C	13	B
4	A	14	C	4	B	14	A
5	B	15	B	5	D	15	A
6	B	16	D	6	C	16	B
7	D	17	C	7	A	17	C
8	D	18	A	8	B	18	40°
9	A	19	D	9	D	19	D
10	182	20	360	10	B	20	B

Practice Test 1

PSSA - Mathematics

Answers and Explanations

1) Answer: B.

5 eggs for 1 cake. Therefore, 260 eggs can be used for (260 ÷ 5) 52 cakes.

2) Answer: A.

Use area of rectangle formula.

Area of a rectangle $= width \times length \Rightarrow D = w \times l \Rightarrow w = \frac{D}{l} = \frac{D}{11}$

3) Answer: D.

To list the fractions from least to greatest, you can convert the fractions to decimal.

$\frac{3}{5} = 0.6; \frac{8}{9} = 0.89; \frac{3}{10} = 0.3; \frac{3}{4} = 0.75; \frac{5}{11} = 0.45$

$\frac{3}{10} = 0.3, \frac{5}{11} = 0.45, \frac{3}{5} = 0.6, \frac{3}{4} = 0.75, \frac{8}{9} = 0.89$

Option D shows the fractions in order from least to greatest.

4) Answer: A.

Plug in 35 for A in the equations. Only option A works.

$A + 35 = 70 \Rightarrow 35 + 35 = 70$

5) Answer: B.

7 multiplied by $\frac{3}{2} = \frac{21}{2} = 10.5$, therefore, only choice B is correct.

6) Answer: B.

Use area and circumference of circle formula.

Area of a circle $= \pi r^2 \Rightarrow 64\pi = \pi r^2 \Rightarrow r = 8$

Circumference of a circle $= 2\pi r \Rightarrow C = 2 \times 8 \times \pi \Rightarrow C = 16\pi$

7) Answer: D.

Use volume of rectangle formula.

Volume of a rectangle$= width \times length \times heigh \Rightarrow V = 7 \times 6 \times 9 \Rightarrow V = 378$

8) Answer: D.

To find the selling price, multiply the price by (100% – rate of discount).

Then: (140) (100% – 15%) = (140) (0.85) = 119

9) Answer: A.

There are 60 cards in the bag and 12 of them are white. Then, 12 out of 60 cards are white. You can write this as: $\frac{12}{60}$. To simplify this fraction, divide both numerator and denominator by 12. Then: $\frac{12}{60} = \frac{1}{5}$

10) Answer: 182.

First, find the missing side of the trapezoid. The perimeter of the trapezoid below is 50.

Therefore, the missing side of the trapezoid (its height) is:

$58 - 12 - 14 - 18 = 58 - 44 = 14$

Area of a trapezoid: $A = \frac{1}{2} h (b1 + b2)$

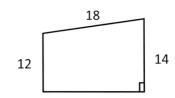

$= \frac{1}{2} (14) (12 + 14) = 182$

11) Answer: C.

1 meter of the rope = 400 grams

14.5 meter of the rope = $14.5 \times 400 = 5{,}800$ grams = 5.8 kg

12) Answer: C.

13 yards = $13 \times 36 = 468$ inches

5 feet = $5 \times 12 = 60$ inches

13 yards 5 feet and 6 inches = 468 inches + 60 inches + 6 inches = 534 inches

13) Answer: A.

Simplify each option provided using order of operations rules.

A. $2 + (-15) - (-8) = 2 - 15 + 8 = -5$

B. $4 + (-2) \times (-5) = 4 + 10 = 14$

C. $-5 \times (-3) + (-4) \times (-10) = 15 + 40 = 54$

D. $3 \times (-5) + 8 = -15 + 8 = -7$

Only option A is -5.

14) Answer: D.

Use percent formula:

$$\text{part} = \frac{\text{percent}}{100} \times \text{whole}$$

$$750 = \frac{\text{percent}}{100} \times 2,500 \Rightarrow 750 = \text{percent} \times 25 \Rightarrow \text{percent} = 30$$

15) Answer: B.

Use area of rectangle formula.

$$\text{Area} = length \times width \Rightarrow A = \frac{3}{8} \times \frac{4}{15} \Rightarrow A = \frac{1}{10} \text{ inches}$$

16) Answer: D.

Write the numbers in order:

7, 16, 16, 19, 21, 24, 32

Median is the number in the middle. Therefore, the median is 19.

17) Answer: C.

$$\frac{1}{3} + \frac{7}{9} - \frac{5}{18} = \frac{(6\times1)+(2\times7)-(1\times5)}{18} = \frac{15}{18} = \frac{5}{6}$$

18) Answer: A.

1 acre: 170 pine trees

20 acres: $170 \times 20 = 3,400$ pine trees

19) Answer: D.

To solve this problem, divide $4\frac{1}{3}$ by $\frac{1}{3}$.

$$4\frac{1}{3} \div \frac{1}{3} = \frac{13}{3} \div \frac{1}{3} = \frac{13}{3} \times \frac{3}{1} = 13$$

20) Answer: 360.

Use volume of cylinder formula.

$$\text{Volume} = base \times heigth \Rightarrow V = 40 \times 9 \Rightarrow V = 360$$

Practice Test 2

PSSA - Mathematics

Answers and Explanations

1) Answer: C.

$15 + (17 \times 21) = 15 + 357 = 372$

2) Answer: D.

1 hour: $3.95

9 hours: $9 \times \$3.95 = \$35.55$

3) Answer: C.

An obtuse angle is an angle of greater than $90°$ and less than $180°$. From the options provided, only option C (130 degrees) is an obtuse angle.

4) Answer: B.

$8 - 4\frac{3}{5} = \frac{40}{5} - \frac{23}{5} = \frac{17}{5} = 3\frac{2}{5}$

5) Answer: D.

The number of guests that are not present are: $(250 - 203)$ 47 out of $230 = \frac{47}{250}$

Change the fraction to percent: $\frac{47}{250} \times 100\% = 18.8\%$

6) Answer: C.

Write a proportion and solve.

$\frac{9 \text{ soft drinks}}{18 \text{ guests}} = \frac{x}{216 \text{ guests}} \Rightarrow x = \frac{216 \times 9}{18} \Rightarrow x = 108$

7) Answer: A.

$\text{average (mean)} = \frac{\text{sum of terms}}{\text{number of terms}} \Rightarrow \text{average} = \frac{6+9+21+24+35+37+37+39}{8} \Rightarrow \text{average} = 26$

8) Answer: B.

Every 120 minutes Emma checks her email.

In 16 hours (960 minutes), Emma checks her email ($960 \div 120$) 8 times.

9) Answer: D.

Divide the number flowers by 12: $492 \div 12 = 41$

10) Answer: B.

Rounding decimals is similar to rounding other numbers. If the hundredths and thousandths places of a decimal is forty-nine or less, they are dropped, and the tenths place does not change. For example, rounding 0.712 to the nearest tenth would give 0.7. Therefore, 5,198.48525 rounded to the nearest tenth is 5,198.5.

11) Answer: D.

Perimeter of rectangle formula:

$$P = 2\,(length + width) \Rightarrow 108 = 2\,(l + 28) \Rightarrow l = 26$$

Area of rectangle formula: $A = length \times width \Rightarrow A = 26 \times 28 \Rightarrow A = 728$

12) Answer: D.

Use volume of rectangle prism formula.

$$V = length \times width \times height \Rightarrow V = 9 \times 3 \times 8 \Rightarrow V = 216$$

13) Answer: B.

The diameter of the circle is 8 inches. Therefore, the radius of the circle is 4 inches.

Use circumference of circle formula.

$C = 2\pi r \Rightarrow C = 2 \times 3.14 \times 4 \Rightarrow C = 25.12$

14) Answer: A.

The line segment is from 8 to -2. Therefore, the line is 10 units.

$$8 - (-2) = 8 + 2 = 10$$

15) Answer: A.

Peter's speed $= \dfrac{140}{7} = 20$

Jason's speed $= \dfrac{300}{6} = 50$

$\dfrac{The\ average\ speed\ of\ peter}{The\ average\ speed\ of\ Jason} = \dfrac{20}{50}$ equals to: $\dfrac{2}{5}$ or $2:5$

16) Answer: B.

Plug in $x = -3$ in each equation.

A. $x(3x - 5) = 45 \rightarrow (-3)(3(-3) - 5) = (-3) \times (-9 - 5) = 42$

B. $5\,(3 - x) = 30 \rightarrow 5(3 - (-3)) = 5(6) = 30$

C. $4\,(2x + 1) = 16 \rightarrow 4(2(-3) + 1) = 4(-6 + 1) = -20$

D.$7x - 4 = -28 \rightarrow 7(-3) - 4 = -21 - 4 = -25$

Only option B.

17) Answer: C.

The horizontal axis in the coordinate plane is called the $x - axis$. The vertical axis is called the $y - axis$. The point at which the two axes intersect is called the origin. The origin is at 0 on the $x - axis$ and 0 on the $y - axis$.

18) Answer: 40°.

All angles in every triangle add up to $180°$. Let x be the angle ABC. Then: $180 = 95 + 45 + x \Rightarrow x = 40°$

19) Answer: D.

In fractions, when denominators increase, the value of fractions decrease and as much as numerators increase, the value of fractions increase. Therefore, the least one of this list is: $\frac{1}{11}$ and the greatest one of this list is: $\frac{1}{4}$

20) Answer: B.

Aria teaches 28 hours for four identical courses. Therefore, she teaches 7 hours for each course. Aria earns $25 per hour. Therefore, she earned $175 ($7 \times 25$) for each course.

"End"

Made in United States
North Haven, CT
29 March 2022

17660973R10087